american knees

american knees

SHAWN WONG

INTRODUCTION BY JEFFREY F. L. PARTRIDGE

UNIVERSITY OF WASHINGTON PRESS

SEATTLE

Copyright © 1995 by Shawn Wong
Originally published in 1995
by Simon & Schuster, New York.
First University of Washington Press
edition published in 2005

Introduction by Jeffrey F. L. Partridge
© 2005 by the University of Washington Press
Printed in the United States of America
Designed by Ashley Saleeba
11 10 09 08 07 06 05   5 4 3 2 1

UNIVERSITY OF WASHINGTON PRESS
www.washington.edu/uwpress

LIBRARY OF CONGRESS CATALOGING-IN-PUBLICATION DATA American knees / Shawn Wong ; introduction by Jeffrey F. L. Partridge. p.   cm.
ISBN 0-295-98496-1 (pbk. : alk. paper)

1. Chinese Americans—Fiction.
2. Interracial dating—Fiction.   3. Dating (Social customs)—Fiction.   4. Chinese American families—Fiction.   I. Title.
PS3573.O583A8   2005
813'.54—dc22   2004029424

The paper used in this publication is acid-free and 90 percent recycled from at least 50 percent post-consumer waste.
It meets the minimum requirements of American National Standard for Information Sciences—Permanence of Paper for Printed Library Materials, ANSI Z39.48—1984. ♾♻

To Vicki Tsuchida, my love

acknowledgments

WITH THIS NEW UNIVERSITY OF WASHINGTON PRESS printing of *American Knees*, I have the opportunity to express my gratitude not only to those who were involved in the original 1995 printing but also to others who have been a part of the ten-year public life of this novel. I am eternally grateful to those who made the original publication of this novel possible with their generous support: the Rockefeller Foundation, for granting me a residency in Bellagio, Italy; and to Gianna Celli, Susan Kanemori, Shaun Olander, Charlotte Oshiro, Trisha Kiyohara, Karen Kodama, and the entire Tsuchida family. For being critical readers, I want to thank Kate Trueblood, Gary Luke, Rebecca Saletan, and Barbara Lowenstein. Thank you to Pat Soden and the University of Washington Press for bringing this novel home.

This book was made possible by the love, support, humor, ideas, and words of: Susan Campbell, Wei Ming Dariotis, Christina Fa, Jeanie Kim, and Marianne Weems. I am grateful for the faith and enthusiasm of Jeff and Janis Chan, Lisa Onodera, Eric Byler, Allison Sie, and John Sie of Starz Productions, who all said, "Let's make this novel into a movie."

And, finally, to Erin and Peter, who make me laugh and feel safe.

Excerpts from *American Knees* first appeared in *Charlie Chan Is Dead*, edited by Jessica Hagedorn, *Chicago Review*, *Before Columbus Review*, and *Essence*. Thank you to Frank Chin for the *Planet of the Apes* quote and to Ishmael Reed for permission to use the keys to Jack London College.

introduction

"CAN'T YOU WRITE A BOOK I CAN READ ON THE BEACH?"
These words—an accusation, really—may well be the seeds of
the novel you have in your hands. Shawn Wong's late wife Vicki
Tsuchida was, like many ordinary readers and students, exasperated with the gravity and the postmodern experimentation of much
contemporary literature—the kind we call, usually with no sense of
irony, "serious fiction." Vicki liked her husband's first novel, *Homebase*, but she felt as if she had to read it with a highlighter in hand
just to follow the postmodern disjunctions of sequence, genre, and
memory.

Shawn Wong answered his wife's tongue-in-cheek jibe with
American Knees, a novel that is alive with humor and the tangled
mess of adult sexual relations. I would not be surprised to find a
copy of the book amidst a beachgoer's belongings, stained with
greasy drips of suntan lotion and littered with grains of sand between its pages. But even this beach-worn copy of *American Knees*
could not have made it through the summer without getting a few
dog-eared corners. Like all good fiction, *American Knees* allows us to
escape into a tantalizing story, while it simultaneously invites us to
examine serious issues—issues of relationships, sex, ethnic identity, racial stereotypes, and personal prejudice in modern America.

American Knees is first and foremost a beautiful and erotic love story. It is a love story about individuals who long desperately to connect with each other, to communicate, to make love and belong to one another—but they often find themselves staring at a gulf between them. Raymond and Aurora's relationship begins with "eye contact" from across a crowded room in Washington, D.C., where they are "the only two Asians at the party." Self-doubt and insecurities cause them to avoid each other, but they somehow know they are going to end up together. The entire party segment is like a dance, as Raymond and Aurora weave near and then pull away, slowly giving in to the inevitable. Aurora hates the idea that all her co-workers must be thinking the two Asians should get together. This strikes her as so stereotypical, so cliché.

And when they do unite, there is a palpable distance between them. Their first intimate act is performed as phone sex with 3,000 miles between them. Even their physical love-making is accompanied by Raymond's erotic narratives that take them to distant places—by the power of imagination removing them from the present as if they knew that their differences in age, ethnicity, and experience could not last in the real world. Raymond fears that "in person the relationship wouldn't survive all the inevitable explanations of his failed marriage, disclaimers about his age, and warnings about the distance between them."

Like us, all the characters of the novel are in search of a fulfilling relationship. Betty Nguyen's pain runs deep, leaving an emotional void that Raymond realizes he could never fill. When Raymond's mother dies, Raymond's father finds himself alone and empty. In one of the most tender scenes of the book, Wood says to Raymond, "I need you to sleep in the bed with me. . . . There's too much space there." That space between people is the real subject of the novel. And so it is fitting that this love story ends in a garden with Raymond and Aurora on opposite sides of a bridge.

The sex gets steamy. But as we wipe the fog from our glasses, we find ourselves gazing into the most intimate questions a person can ask. Who am I? Who are you? In the first chapter of the novel, we are introduced to Raymond Ding, a man who is suffering a peculiar kind of divorce, for it is a divorce not just from his wife but from his ethnic identity. Married to Darleen, Raymond's ethnic identity was solidly fixed: he was the son-in-law of a true Chinese patriarch who ran his restaurants modeled on Confucian ideals of filial piety and selfless service to the family enterprise. In Darleen's family, Raymond was the dutiful Chinese son. He did not need to establish his identity; he simply wore it like a tailor-made suit. The divorce strips him of that Chinese-son feeling, leaving him to comment sardonically, "I used to be Chinese, but my wife got custody of my ethnicity."

(I can almost hear a voice calling above the din of the crashing waves: "Honey, remind me to throw a few highlighters in with the beach towels next time, okay?")

In a sense, Raymond converts from "Chinese" to "Asian American" after his divorce. Raymond was "a good Chinese boy" growing up, and he fulfilled "his legendary Chinese filial duty" by marrying into a Chinese family. The distinction for Raymond is clear: his role managing a Chinese restaurant for his father-in-law is the "inside" and the rest of society is "outside." His father-in-law even bases Raymond's salary on what he would make "in the 'outside' world," suggesting that Darleen's family is somehow segregated from the rest of America. The business practices, personal relationships, and expectations are all Chinese. Now, divorced from Darleen and her Chinese world, Raymond must find his way in that "outside world," an America that taunted him on the playgrounds of his youth, asking him with mock slanted eyes, "What are you—Chinese, Japanese, or American Knees?"

Unlike many Asian American books that begin with the protagonist's search for self-identity from adolescence, or which trace personal lineage through the upheavals of immigration, *American Knees* sets its protagonist adrift in adulthood. With no wreckage to cling to from his sunken marriage, Raymond clings to the most tangible identity he can find: a rigid and almost militant belief in the necessity of ethnic pride. Raymond riles at America's past injustices toward Asian Americans, and he works diligently for the leveling of the playing field in his role as director of minority affairs at Jack London College. The name of the college is Wong's ironic dig at Raymond and his newfound mission; the college that pays him to fight for minority rights is named after a man who once called the Chinese race "the menace of the western world."[1] Raymond grounds his new ethnic identity in the lessons of Asian American history—the exploitation of Chinese laborers in building the Union Pacific Railroad, the internment of Japanese Americans during World War II, the legal exclusion (by act of Congress) of Chinese immigrants from 1882 to the 1940s, and the racist representation of Asians in pulp fiction and films.

Raymond's discussion with his friend Jimmy Chan about a 1930s pulp novel called *Chinese Girls in Bondage* exemplifies Raymond's cognizance of the injustices of the Asian American past. Raymond and Jimmy poke fun at the novel's characterization of "Chinamen" who "lived in rat-infested tunnels" under Chinatown's streets, smoked opium, and "sold their women into slavery":

"Why were we selling our women," [Raymond asks].
"They were being sold into prostitution," [says Jimmy].
"Why didn't we just be the pimps? Isn't that more profitable in the long run?"
"We were stupid and evil."
"And why would we sell Chinese girls? Wouldn't we want to keep them? There weren't any Chinese women around then."

Raymond is right about the ahistorical underpinnings of the pulp novel's stereotypes. Even if these "Chinamen" were diabolical enough to sell their women, the plain historical fact is that there were precious few Chinese women in the Chinatowns of the early twentieth century. Because the Chinese Exclusion Act of 1882 prevented Chinese men already living in America from sending for wives or "picture brides" from their homeland, the Chinatowns of America became known as "bachelor societies." There were also miscegenation laws in many states that prohibited the marriage of Asians and whites. In California, the legal ban against interracial marriage was overturned by the United States Supreme Court in 1948, but it wasn't until 1967 that the Supreme Court declared all miscegenation laws unconstitutional. As is usually true with racial stereotypes, the facts of history that Raymond cites are simply overshadowed by a spirit of prejudice. Jimmy's response to Raymond's barrage of questions makes this clear: "It's pulp fiction from the thirties. It was written by a white guy. Evil Chinamen are evil Chinamen, plain and simple. We sell women. We live in tunnels in Chinatown."

The plot description of the fictitious *Chinese Girls in Bondage* is modeled on popular novels such as Sax Rohmer's Fu-Manchu series, first published in 1911, that mined the deep vein of "yellow horde" paranoia in American society. The idea of the yellow horde, or yellow peril, is founded on a popular American belief that the Chinese and other Asians are an insidious threat to the nation. According to the stereotype, Asians are mysterious, sly, untrustworthy, inherently evil, and as populous as a swarm of insects. This is how Fu-Manchu is described in Rohmer's *The Insidious Dr. Fu-Manchu*:

Imagine a person, tall, lean and feline, high-shouldered, with a brow like Shakespeare and a face like Satan, a close-shaven skull, and long, mag-

netic eyes of the true cat-green. Invest him with all the cruel cunning of an
entire Eastern race, accumulated in one giant intellect, with all the resources of science past and present, with all the resources, if you will, of a
wealthy government--which, however, already has denied all knowledge
of his existence. Imagine that awful being, and you have a mental picture
of Dr. Fu-Manchu, the yellow peril incarnate in one man.[2]

Rohmer did not invent the yellow peril any more than Jack London
did. What he asks us to imagine in the above description assumes
that we already believe in the "cruel cunning of an entire Eastern
race." This xenophobic attitude toward Asians produced more than
trashy and racist fiction; it is the same attitude that led the
American government to restrict Asian immigration in contrast to
European immigration (e.g., The Chinese Exclusion Act of 1882),
to exclude Asian residents from the right of citizenship (e.g., The
National Origins Act of 1924), and even to deny Asian citizens their
freedom (e.g., Executive Order 9066 in 1942, which led to the internment of 112,000 Japanese Americans).

On the other hand, while Raymond's Asian American sensibility
may be grounded in Asian American history, his daily experience is
grounded in the realities of post-1965 Asian America. The world
of *American Knees* reflects the changes in American demography
since the United States Congress passed the Immigration Act in
1965. The Immigration Act abolished the immigration quotas established by the 1924 National Origins Act that had for decades
reduced legal Asian immigration to a trickle. The 1965 Immigration Act, coupled with American involvement in Asian con-
flicts in Korea and Vietnam, opened the door to greater numbers
of Asian immigrants and a concomitant increase in the diversity of
Asian ethnicities among immigrants. The world "outside" Darleen's Chinese family reflects this diversity. Jimmy Chan and

Brenda Nishitani are American-born Chinese and Japanese, respectively. Raymond's father is also American-born, but Raymond's late mother is an immigrant from China. Aurora Crane is the daughter of an American-born Japanese woman and a white father who served in Korea during the Korean War.

But it is Raymond's relationship with Betty Nguyen that best illustrates the contrasts between pre- and post-1965 Asian America. In many respects, we might expect Raymond to have more in common with Betty than he does with Aurora. Betty is Raymond's age and thus shares the same generational experiences: as Betty puts it, they "know the words to the same songs from the seventies." Betty, like Raymond, has experienced the traumas of divorce. She is also one hundred percent Asian, as is Raymond. Aurora, on the other hand, is more than ten years younger than Raymond and has inherited enough of her father's looks and the upper-Midwest culture of her childhood to "pass" as white when she wishes. The irony is that Raymond and Betty, while looking the part of the Asian couple who have everything in common, are in fact culturally worlds apart. Raymond's childhood stories are "classically American and utterly unfamiliar" to Betty: his scars come from falling off his bicycle, but Betty's past bears the scars, both mental and physical, of poverty, of the Vietnam war, of her experiences as a refugee, and of an abusive relationship. Betty's Vietnamese American experience differs dramatically from Raymond's American-born Chinese experience, giving the lie to stereotypical American assumptions that Asians are all alike and revealing the barriers that often impede understanding among a diverse Asian American population.

Ethnic identity is treated with complexity in *American Knees*. The characters adopt a variety of postures that suggest there are multiple ways to conceive of one's ethnic identity. Brenda Nishitani refuses to acknowledge an Asian American identity; Aurora discovers through Raymond that she needs to embrace an Asian American identity; Betty cannot escape her Vietnamese immigrant identity; and Raymond learns by the end of the novel that his rigid approach to Asian American identity needs some softening around the edges. Through Aurora and Raymond, the novel suggests that identity is not a stable essence that an individual discovers but an ongoing, creative process.

Shawn Wong has contributed greatly to the development of contemporary Asian American literature, and a brief sketch of his career as a writer, anthologist, and teacher is almost analogous to a sketch of Asian American literature's growth from birth to adulthood. As an English major and aspiring writer at UC Berkeley in the late 1960s, Wong realized that he knew of no other Asian American authors, no Asian American literary tradition, no works that he could look to as a path to the present. Wong explained in an interview,

I was 19 or 20 years old and I was writing pretty bad poetry. I thought it was good poetry, but like a lot of beginning poets it was very abstract and highly sentimental. I was experimenting. This was around 1969, at Berkeley, during all the riots and the beginnings of ethnic studies. I realized one day that I was the only Asian American writer I knew in the world. It just dawned on me one day: "I'm trying to be a writer—why is it I don't know any other Asian American writers? Why hasn't a teacher ever assigned an Asian American book, or even mentioned one?" So I went to my professors at Berkeley and asked them, and they couldn't name anyone.[3]

We know today that the Asian American literary tradition extends back to the nineteenth century, but our knowledge of this owes much to the work of Wong and his colleagues. Wong soon teamed up with Frank Chin and Jeffery Paul Chan, and later Lawson Fusao

Inada, to discover lost and forgotten works by Asian American writers. They found *Yokohama, California* (1949) in a used bookstore and tracked down the author, Toshio Mori. Mori, then well along in years, gave them copies of stories, some of which he had written when he was living in an internment camp during World War II. "It was a real find for us," says Wong. "Here was this wonderful book of stories about Japanese Americans in the San Francisco Bay area prior to World War II. We thought, 'Somebody did come before us and somebody did try to write about the same kind of issues that we're struggling with.'"[4]

As more and more Asian American works came into their hands, they realized the best way to share their discoveries was to produce an anthology. The result was *Aiiieeeee! An Anthology of Asian American Writers*, which was published by Howard University Press in 1974. The anthology included works from the new-found tradition by Carlos Bulosan, Diana Chang, Louis Chu, Hisaye Yamamoto, and Wakako Yamauchi, and new works by the editors and other writers. By this time, Chan and Wong had already started teaching what they believe to be the nation's first Asian American literature class at San Francisco State University, where Wong began his master's degree studies in Creative Writing in 1971.

While the publication of forgotten and new Asian American creative voices in *Aiiieeeee!* had a profound impact on the development of Asian American literature in the 1970s and beyond, it is the four editors' introductory essay to the volume and the preface to the 1991 Mentor edition that stirred up the most controversy. Many critics fault the editors for a male-centered outlook that borders on the misogynist, and some scholars criticize the editors for placing narrow boundaries on the definition of Asian American literature. King-Kok Cheung believes Chin, Chan, Inada, and Wong "discounted the work of most foreign-born Asians and discredited the bicultural tension that often does surface in literature by both immigrant and American-born writers."[5] Cheung faults the editors with placing rigid restrictions on Asian American literary expression and diversity, especially Frank Chin in his scathing and hyperbolic essay for The Big Aiiieeeee! (1991), "Come All Ye Asian American Writers of the Real and Fake." Cheung writes, "these editors, so instrumental in launching the literature, have subsequently vilified much of it by arbitrating what is 'real' and what is 'fake' Asian American writing."[6]

The "Real and Fake" essay is a highly polemical attack on writers such as Maxine Hong Kingston, Amy Tan, and David Henry Hwang, accusing them of feminizing Asians and appealing to white stereotypes of the mystical, misogynist, superstitious "Oriental." The essay was originally intended to carry the names of all four editors, but when Wong, Chan, and Inada read Chin's draft, they agreed that it was really his voice and that it should go into The Big Aiiieeeee! as Frank Chin's essay.[7] This fact draws a distinction between Shawn Wong's approach to Asian American literature and Frank Chin's approach. As with Chin's fiction, both Homebase and American Knees develop father/son and male/female relationships that challenge the stereotypes of the patriarchal, misogynist Chinese male. Wong even pokes fun at Amy Tan in American Knees when a white man who believes all the stereotypes raves about this wonderful new novel, Lucknow Nights Without Joy in Chinatown, which plays on the title of Tan's famous book, The Joy Luck Club. "Man, what a tearjerker," the man says, "when Mei-mei and her mother triumph over the vicious cycle of Chinese misogyny and despair." Raymond, by contrast, "could not get past the first chapter." But in interviews and other essays, Wong has shown none of the acerbity that characterizes Frank Chin's discourse. In interviews, Chin has called Kingston a "fool" and a "white racist" who "treats Chinese America as if it is hers to invent."[8] Yet, in spite of Chin's over-the-top rhetoric, or perhaps *because* of it, the Chin-Kingston feud has done much to enliven the field of Asian American literature. Kingston even responded to Chin's anger by characterizing him as Wittman Ah Sing, the protagonist of her novel, *Tripmaster Monkey*. Wittman is a hot-headed Chinese American who gets offended at whites and other Chinese Americans but eventually learns to get along.

Even the most trenchant critics of Chin and the other *Aiiieeeee!* editors credit them with energizing the debate and defining its issues. "It was Frank Chin and his associates," writes Sau-ling Cynthia Wong, "who, in their prefatory essays affirming cultural dynamism, set forth most of the terms of debate on what counts as Chinese American literature. Controversial as these views are, they represent the first clear articulation of the possibilities of a Chinese American literary identity."[9] And despite her ideological disagreements with them, King-Kok Cheung calls the *Aiiieeeee!* editors "socially committed forerunners" who were "instrumental in securing the freedom and diversity of expression enjoyed by Asian American writers at present."[10] Understood in the context of the civil rights era, the introduction to *Aiiieeeee!* is an impassioned indictment of American racism toward Asians and a pronouncement of Asian American independence at a time when the Asian American community needed it most.

In 1969, Wong, along with Frank Chin, Jeffery Chan, and Lawson Inada formed the Combined Asian-American Resources Project (CARP). CARP was instrumental in recovering many texts that are now taught in Asian American literature classes as standard classics of the Asian American literary tradition, and the University of Washington Press played the primary role in republishing these works. Carlos Bulosan's *America Is in the Heart* (1946) was reissued in 1973, John Okada's *No-No Boy* (1957) in 1976, Louis Chu's *Eat a Bowl* of *Tea* (1961) in 1979, and Monica Sone's *Nisei Daughter* (1953) also in 1979. *Yokohama, California*, originally published in 1949, is currently available in its 1985 reprint edition by the University of Washington Press, with an introduction by Lawson Inada.

Wong published his first novel, *Homebase*, in 1979, three years after moving to Seattle, Washington, where he teaches as a professor in the English Department of the University of Washington. The novel won a Pacific Northwest Booksellers Award and a Washington State Governor's Writers Award and is still available today. In her groundbreaking 1982 study, *Asian American Literature: An Introduction to the Writings and Their Social Contexts*, Elaine H. Kim calls *Homebase* "a triumphant reaffirmation of the Chinese American heritage" that "ends with a reconciliation between father and son, who are linked by their American roots."[11] In the sixteen years separating his first and second novel, Wong edited several important anthologies, including *The Before Columbus Foundation Poetry/ Fiction Anthology* (1992), co-edited with Ishmael Reed, Gundars Strads, and Kathryn Trueblood, an anthology of Asian American literature for Harper/Collins (1996), and *The Big Aiiieeeee!* (1991).

When *American Knees* was published in 1995, the Asian American literary landscape was dramatically different from the way it appeared to a twenty-year-old undergraduate at UC Berkeley in 1969. In just twenty-five years, Asian American literature had emerged from total obscurity to notoriety and acclaim. Today, universities throughout the United States and overseas offer courses on Asian American literature, and many universities have Asian American centers and programs. Books by Asian Americans abound in bookstores and many appear on bestseller lists. Asian American writers have claimed such coveted prizes as the National Book Award, the PEN/Faulkner Award, and the Pulitzer. It is fitting that a man who had so much to do with the birth of Asian American literature as we know it has given us the novel of its adulthood. Even considering all that Shawn Wong has done for Asian American literature as a researcher, anthologist, and professor, *American Knees* is perhaps his greatest contribution: it is the book of the Asian American present that has not forgotten the Asian American past.

JEFFREY F. L. PARTRIDGE

January 2005

Notes

1. Jack London. "The Yellow Peril." *Revolution and other Essays*. New York: MacMillan, 1910, p. 281.
2. Sax Rohmer. *The Insidious Fu-Manchu*. 1913. Mineola, NY: Dover, 1997, p. 13.
3. Jeffrey F. L. Partridge. "Aiiieeeee! and the Asian American Literary Movement: A Conversation with Shawn Wong." MELUS 29.3 &4 (Fall & Winter 2004), p. 92.
4. Ibid., p. 94.
5. King-Kok Cheung, ed. *An Interethnic Companion to Asian American Literature*. Cambridge: Cambridge University Press, 1997, p. 2.
6. Ibid., p. 11.
7. Jeffrey F. L. Partridge. "Aiiieeeee! and the Asian American Literary Movement: A Conversation with Shawn Wong." MELUS 29.3 & 4 (Fall & Winter 2004), p. 96.
8. Nina Morgan and Jachison Chan. "In Defense of the Real: Frank Chin in Dialogue." *The Diasporic Imagination: Asian American Writing, Vol. 1*. Somdatta Mandel, ed. New Delhi: Prestige Books, 1999, p. 51.
9. Sau-ling Cynthia Wong. "Chinese American Literature." *An Interethnic Companion to Asian American Literature*. King-Kok Cheung, ed. Cambridge: Cambridge University Press, 1997, p. 40.
10. King-Kok Cheung, ed. *An Interethnic Companion to Asian American Literature*. Cambridge: Cambridge University Press, 1997, p. 17.
11. Elaine H. Kim. *Asian American Literature: An Introduction to the Writings and Their Social Context*. Philadelphia: Temple University Press, 1982, p. 194.

american knees

1   loyalty, betrayal, & revenge

"YOU WON'T EVEN BE CHINESE AFTER YOUR WIFE'S attorney gets through with you, Raymond," Sylvia Beacon-Yamaki said, flipping the pages of Darleen's proposed divorce settlement. Raymond wondered if someone could be a lapsed Chinese, in the same way people become lapsed Catholics. If Darleen took away her family from him and he ceased having the opportunity to be the dutiful Chinese son, would that make him a lapsed Chinese? Raymond made a mental note to ask his Jewish friend, Sam, who was one of those legendary good-boy Jewish sons and who had recently divorced a dark-haired Jewish woman to marry a blond Catholic woman.

What good was a good Chinese son without a Chinese family in which to practice his legendary Chinese filial duty? What would Raymond do—go around telling people, "Hi, my name is Raymond Ding. I used to be Chinese, but my wife got custody of my ethnicity"? Raymond wondered if this was cultural diversity at its worst.

Raymond Ding's Chinese name translated into English was like all Chinese boys' names were supposed to be—something grandiose and epic, like the name given to a hole-in-the-wall Chinese greasy spoon nestled at a crowded intersection, with chipped Formica tables and unmatched duct-taped Naugahyde chairs. New

Golden Gardens. Golden River Palace. Riverside Palace Inn. Chinese restaurants are not called "Bob's Place." Name and fortune are related. Raymond's name told a tale of a brave warrior, truthful and loyal to his fellow warriors and the gods, a strong foundation, a fortress of shining light, majestic mountain peaks, a fast car with a 7/70 warranty and a lifetime Die Hard battery. This truthful, loyal, and brave one would marry, and his wife would bear him male children so that his name would be passed on to the next generation. *We are immortal*, the family name implied. Actually, Raymond didn't know what his Chinese name was, the name his grandmother had called him in a language he forgot a year after he started public school.

Perhaps not being Chinese was an option in America. Certainly it was easy enough to change your mind and decide to be some other Asian ethnicity, such as Japanese, Korean, Vietnamese, Thai, Cambodian, Malaysian, or even a different kind of Chinese, such as Taiwanese. What non-Asian would know? Or Raymond could even be Chinese from Little Rock, Arkansas, where folks would refer to him as "Say, Ray—Ray Bob Daing" and his accent would mark him unmistakably as American. He had once met a Korean immigrant who had learned English in North Carolina. Her talk was, for the most part, perfect English—some confusion with r's and l's, an occasional h thrown in behind an a, and a wandering accent on polysyllabic words that made her sound like Nancy Kwan in *The World of Suzie Wong*, with Richard Petty as her English teacher. But when she drawled, people knew she was an American. When Raymond spoke, with no accent, they just noticed that he spoke pretty good English. In the schoolyard, kids used to taunt him. "What are you— Chinese, Japanese, or American Knees?" they'd chant, slanting the corners of their eyes up and down, displaying a bucktoothed smile, and pointing at their knees. When Raymond, not liking any of the choices, didn't answer, they'd say, "Then you must be dirty knees."

◆ ◆ ◆

SYLVIA BEACON-YAMAKI was one of those hyphenated-by-marriage women. Raymond concluded from her name that she liked Asian men and therefore would not be too judgmental about any failures on his part when she exercised her duty as his attorney. He had met her when they volunteered at an art auction to raise funds for an Asian community mental health clinic. Now, six months later, he had appeared at her office after five, without an appointment. He didn't know any other attorneys.

She remembered him. She ushered him in, took off her blazer, kicked off her shoes, and motioned for him to sit next to her at the conference table. When Raymond uttered the words "My wife, Darleen, and I are getting divorced. I might need your help," Sylvia realized he was seated too close, her blouse was too tight, her skirt too short. He placed the opposing attorney's settlement papers on the table in front of her and stared at the floor. Was he looking at her red toenails? "I've got a couple of beers in the refrigerator," she said. It was the right thing to say. In the office kitchen, under the fluorescent lights, Sylvia read the proposed settlement and Raymond explained his marriage.

DARLEEN'S FIRST WORDS to him had been "Say, Ray." When he looked back on that moment, he wanted to offer others this advice: "Never marry your first Chinese girlfriend." Raymond, at thirty, had just finished his graduate degree in public administration at Berkeley. Darleen, at twenty-six, had an M.B.A. degree and was working for a bank while she studied for the CPA exam. Her roommate was a classmate of Raymond's and had convinced Darleen that the Asian guys in the public administration program were less nerdy than the ones in the business school. After a meeting of a minority students' coalition, the three of them went to a

Chinese restaurant, where Darleen ordered in Cantonese. The owner of the restaurant knew her father and didn't charge them. Darleen insisted on paying and left a twenty-dollar bill on the table, but the owner ran after her and gave her a bag of lichee candy, in which Darleen later discovered her twenty-dollar bill. The food, the money, the family honor, were played out to perfection in a classic Chinese morality play.

Raymond recognized all the right cultural signals. Darleen and her family would give him the large Chinese American family he'd never had. Her two older brothers and sisters had already married, in order of birth. He and Darleen would be the next. They would fall in love, get married, and have children—preferably male children—who would be given fabulous red-egg parties on their one-month birthdays. Raymond moved to West Covina, a suburb east of Los Angeles, to join the family and be Chinese. He felt lucky. Believing in luck and fate was very Chinese.

DARLEEN'S FATHER OWNED two upscale Chinese restaurants that catered to a white clientele. While Raymond was looking for a job in public administration, Darleen's father offered to let him be the night manager at General Chan's Palace restaurant. After all, Raymond had real college training in administration, employee relations, and management. Raymond tried to explain that his training was more in the public sector, specifically in issues relating to affirmative action and human rights. Darleen's father puffed on his cigar. "Perfect! We serve the public." Raymond thought managing a small minority-owned business right out of graduate school couldn't hurt his résumé. Things fell into place.

Raymond had left the restaurant a couple of times, once to become an affirmative action officer at a community college, then later to work as an investigator for Orange County's Department of Human Rights, but he lost both jobs to budget cut-backs. Each time he came back to the restaurant, and each time Darleen's father matched his salary in the "outside" world.

It was as if at the exact moment he married Darleen, whoever oversaw good Chinese boys had tapped him on the shoulder and said, "Son, your time has come. Follow me. Your dead mother would have wanted it this way." Ancestors for seventy-five generations back had nodded in agreement. "Good boy, good boy, good boy," they had chanted as he was led away.

Away. That was the key to the whole matter: away from what? Raymond knew exactly what he had given up and what he had been led away from. For Darleen, the marriage had been something she was directed to, a destination, the beginning of a life branching out in all directions from the common root of their union. But Raymond was already perched on the tip of one of the branches, and the ancestors were sawing it off and planting it in the ground, saying, "Good boy. Grow new roots and we'll forget about your girlfriends who weren't Chinese. You didn't know what you were doing. You were young. Too much rock and roll."

"Too moochie moobies," as Grandma would say about the grandson who strayed too far.

Loretta Young was the only white woman Grandma approved of. She watched *The Loretta Young Show* every week on television, and she never forgot that earlier in her career, Loretta Young had saved Chinese orphans and fought Japs with Alan Ladd in the movie *China*. In *The Hatchet Man*, Loretta Young *was* a Chinese daughter, her eyes taped and latexed into an "Oriental" slant. Edward G. Robinson was the tong hatchet man who was ordered to kill her father—who happened to be Edward G. Robinson's good friend—because he betrayed the tong. Friendship was one thing, but betrayal was a whole other thing. Before chopping his friend's head off, Edward G. Robinson promised to raise Loretta Young as if she were his daughter. Business was business, and a promise was a promise. In the end, all Chinese stories came down to loyalty, betrayal, and revenge.

Things fell into place until Darleen's father became Burl Ives and Darleen became Elizabeth Taylor and Raymond became Paul Newman in *Cat on a Hot Tin Roof*. Raymond realized what Darleen's brothers had known all their lives—in a family business, there is no free will. The only freedom Darleen's father offered her brothers was to give them their own restaurant to manage. They were destined to work in the restaurant business whether they wanted to or not. One of them once said to Raymond, "If I weren't paying myself such a high salary, I'd quit." But you couldn't quit family.

The freedom Raymond's father had given him as an only child hadn't prepared him for working within the patriarchy of a large Chinese family business. Neither had his studies in public administration prepared him; the courses he would have needed were all in the psychology department. In Darleen's family Raymond became just another son, another brother. He had no other social life.

His life at the restaurant became separate from Darleen's life and from their life together. At work under bright lights, his life was on constant display, surrounded by background music, the constant chatter bouncing off the walls as he moved between tables, and the metallic and ceramic noise of the kitchen. He came home after closing, craving a darkened and silent anonymity, and moved about the house without turning on the lights. Sometimes he pretended he was alone and unmarried. He stopped cooking for himself and Darleen, stopped eating meals at home, stopped listening to music, and watched television with the sound off. He never answered the phone; any call at home was for Darleen.

She was comfortable with Raymond's silence, which was just like her brothers'. Her brothers never spoke of work because it seemed they had been working and living in the restaurant for their entire lives. Darleen had an M.B.A. degree and a CPA license and had written a master's thesis on minority businesswomen who had received loans from the Small Business Administration, yet there was no place for her in the family business. She worked for a bank, in the commercial loan division. She understood that the power in the family rested on the shoulders of the men. This wasn't the legendary and oppressive Chinese patriarchy at work; it was freedom and the luxury of choice for Darleen.

In order to prevent arguments, Raymond avoided discussing work at home, because any dissatisfaction with work meant a dissatisfaction with the family. To express dissatisfaction meant he was an ungrateful Chinese son-in-law.

"The cooks don't listen to me, Darleen."

"You don't speak Cantonese."

"They understand English when your father speaks to them in English."

"He's the boss."

"What am I?"

"The son-in-law."

"Worse. The boss's youngest daughter's husband."

"You should be grateful Daddy pays you the same as you get on the outside."

"On the outside," Raymond thought, had a familiar ring to it: *Stalag 17*, perhaps, or *What Ever Happened to Baby Jane?*

His past was equally dangerous conversation, because everything he had done in his adult life, he had done with another woman. All his postpuberty experiences in Los Angeles were tainted with the company of former girlfriends. Darleen wanted him separated from them. At first her jealousy was amusing. Then it was not amusing. If he admitted to having been to UCLA or Newport Beach, or mentioned a couple of nice restaurants in Venice Beach, an interrogation would follow, or stony silence. He learned to control the urge to participate in conversations that required him to relate experiences other than childhood ones. A casual listener might have surmised that as an adult he had seen no movies, taken no vacations, had no girlfriends before Darleen. He would have admitted to going to Disneyland as a child, but no one in Los Angeles ever asked about that.

"I WISH I WERE MARRIED TO LORETTA YOUNG," Raymond muttered. He paused. Sylvia Beacon-Yamaki waited. He had barely mentioned the usual subjects of divorce—money, infidelity, sex. Not that there hadn't been any infidelity.

One day a red-haired wine rep wearing a dress with a zipper from the neckline to the hemline had stepped into the restaurant office with two bottles of wine, introduced herself, apologized for being late (she was supposed to meet with Darleen's father, but Raymond didn't enlighten her), sat down at Raymond's desk (it was her last appointment of the day), slipped off her high heels, and asked if he knew any of "that Oriental acupressure stuff."

Raymond was a good Chinese boy who never cut class, always had the proper letter from home, kept his gym clothes clean, returned his library books on time, never tore up a parking ticket, didn't burn his draft card, wrote thank you letters the day after Christmas and the day after his birthday, never ran out of gas, took driver's ed, asked about birth control at the proper time, kept written warranties in a safe place, and had inhaled only ten times, at a party.

He looked the wine rep in the eyes and lied. In order for it to be done right, she'd have to take off her panty hose, "so that negative ions flowing outward won't be blocked." He threw in something about the Yangtze River flowing to the sea. She had green eyes. She wasn't wearing panties. An unexcused absence requires a note from home. Void where prohibited. He removed the tag under penalty of law.

In her Venice Beach apartment, miles from West Covina and General Chan's Palace, Raymond became fascinated with her pubic hairs, a mound of very tiny, tight red curls. He ran his fingers through them, straightening them, then released them and watched them bounce back into tiny curls. After that there were freckles to count.

He began to keep a bathrobe at her place. She rented an extra parking slot. There was a sudden public administration conference out of town. On another occasion, he gave a waitress a ride home sixteen nights in a row. His life, which had become so separate from Darleen's, was no longer equal.

Given Darleen's jealousy, it didn't take her long to discover his infidelity. Suddenly he knew his way around Venice Beach without asking for directions, he remembered the plots of recent movies they hadn't seen together, he revealed a newfound knowledge of vintage wine. *Exhibit A, Your Honor*—*red hair and a phone number next to the notation "15,237 freckles" in place of a name.* Bad Chinese son. In the end, the infidelity itself was incidental to the drama of Raymond's disloyalty to and eventual divorce from the family. Technically, it needed the betrayal or it wouldn't have been a complete Chinese tale.

In the movie version of his life, Raymond is seated on a three-legged stool in a gray Cultural Revolution-era prison uniform, his politically correct autobiography in hand. The men in charge of his reeducation are seated at the far end of the room. They all look vaguely like the cooks from General Chan's Palace. Raymond begins to read the twenty-ninth revision of his confession.

I have betrayed the nation-state and lived a selfish life of avarice. I have proven myself ungrateful and unfilial by immersing myself in wanton plea-sures outside the boundaries of the nation-state....

He reads for three days without sleeping, and at the end the men organize a tribunal where they will decide whether Raymond should be sent out to (1) plant rice, (2) break big rocks into little ones, or (3) carry his dick in a jar in public.

As Sylvia continued reading in silence, Raymond thought of the television footage of tanks pushing and clanking into Tiananmen Square. He wanted to be the lone man facing a line of tanks. To be heroic in battle. In the end, all he wanted to do was step aside and let his wife's tank push by while he shouted, "Take everything! Take everything!" He resisted the urge to blame someone else for his divorce and the pitiful bargaining position he had placed himself in.

Chinese actually believed in good luck, happiness, long life, and other phrases forged in steel and dipped in gold and used to decorate Chinese restaurants and the front of bright-red wedding invitations. To ensure all this good fortune, they backed up their good wishes with cash and jewelry at the appropriate times. Weddings and the births of baby boys were big cash days in couples' lives. When someone died, fake paper money was burned and food was offered to the dead to guarantee a journey without hardship. One did not burn real money; Chinese might be superstitious, but they weren't stupid.

Divorce was another kind of death, Raymond thought as he stared at a line in the settlement agreement marked "Loans." Each sum corresponded to a monetary gift from Darleen's family—on their wedding day, at New Year's, on their birthdays, and other holidays. As supporting evidence, copies of canceled checks bearing Raymond's name were attached. Darleen was utilizing her CPA training to full advantage. In his next life he would take cash only or fake money.

Later, in Raymond's only angry moment during the divorce, he returned every gift Darleen and her family had given him during their marriage. No item was too insignificant or too trivial. In fact, the more trivial, the better. He returned T-shirts, slippers he'd never worn, an electric shaver, sweaters, socks, old magazines, shirts, suits, shoes, a half bottle of aspirin, ugly boxer shorts, books, records, tools, anything he had taken with him when they separated that could possibly be construed as a gift. Then, for all the food he had eaten at their restaurants, he bought Darleen and her family a gift certificate to a competing establishment. He had already left behind all the furniture, artwork, towels, kitchen utensils, dishes, pots and pans—everything except what he'd had when he graduated from college and moved to Los Angeles. After he had deposited all the cartons on Darleen's doorstep, he left a note saying, "I'm returning the things you 'loaned' me." He felt unencumbered and less fearful about his failure.

SYLVIA CLOSED THE SETTLEMENT AGREEMENT. "They're burying you."

"She and that attorney of hers, Tasmanian Wombat, can have everything," Raymond muttered.

"Then you'll need a backhoe operator, not an attorney," said Sylvia.

A good Chinese son would automatically have said at this point, "I don't want to hurt her family." What did a man look like after having been run over by a tank?

"If you give them everything, will Darleen's family like you more, Raymond?" Sylvia asked.

If I gave them a discount on my half of the community property, they'd like me more, Raymond thought to himself. Getting a discount was more Chinese. "Let's give them my fifty percent of the community property and discount it by an additional twenty-five percent. And throw in a case of toilet paper."

Sylvia smiled. "If you want a lawyer, then let me be your lawyer." It was the equivalent of a car salesman saying, "What will it take for us to make a deal?"

RAYMOND NAVIGATED the divorce proceedings relatively smoothly, even when he discovered Darleen's attorney's car in her garage at three o'clock in the morning. Sylvia immediately had the lawyer's presence in the about-to-be-disputed community property documented by a private investigator for two weeks, in case the divorce went to trial.

He got his revenge later, when Darleen's attorney took a deposition that Sylvia would use with students for years as an example of how not to take a deposition. The highlight of the transcript was Raymond's proposal that Darleen be given custody of his restaurant knowledge and that he be allowed to patronize Chinese dining establishments only on alternate weekends. Sylvia had to call a break from time to time just to escape to the hallway and laugh. The humiliation, on the record, of his wife's attorney ended up costing Raymond real dollars later, but it was worth it. In fact, he ended up having to turn over the entire settlement check to Sylvia for attorney's fees, but he spoke fondly of winning the battle of wits, if not the war.

After that, Darleen mounted an international telephone campaign, insisting to every friend they had in common that there was a choice to make and that the choice, after the evidence was heard, would be her. Raymond's silence was a guilty plea. No one called to say, "Say, Ray, we're sorry about the divorce, and we know there's always two sides to every story. Let's stay friends." He hated it when people said, "Say, Ray."

Then it was over. Raymond and Darleen's seven-year marriage had come to an end.

2   gold spike

AFTER HIS DIVORCE, RAYMOND MOVED BACK TO THE BAY
Area, where his father still lived. An ominous unspoken thought
descended between them: Raymond would never again marry a
Chinese woman and would thus be the first in his thin branch of
the family tree not to be married to a Chinese. He was already the
first to divorce.

Raymond's father's name was Woodrow, or, as his friends called
him, Wood. His immigrant parents named him after a President, as
they did his brothers, Abraham and Theodore, also American born,
as if their American names could guarantee greatness and wealth.

Did a search for identity have to have symbolic momentum? Was
it enough to push "deep" into the heart of America in a romantic
search for identity, or was it enough to find something somewhere
on the surface, a momentary acknowledgment of a specific time
and place? Perhaps even the faded glory of an American lie would
suffice, the driving of the gold spike to signal the completion of the
transcontinental railroad built by Chinese workers from west to
east, and from east to west by Irish workers—though no Chinese
were allowed in the historic photo of two locomotives meeting at
Promontory Point, Utah. The men holding guns in the photo kept
the Chinese at bay. Raymond's father had told him this version of

American history, yet when he was in school he could not find any mention of it. "Grandpa said it was so," his father had said.

Wood and his two brothers were a rarity, all born in the late twenties in New York's Chinatown, a Chinatown that was still reeling from the effects of immigration laws, a Chinatown of aging bachelors. America liked to call them sojourners, because it meant they wanted eventually to return home. But if this was true, why did America need over a dozen different exclusionary immigration laws, and why did several states pass antimiscegenation and alien land laws? A second generation of bachelors were dying out as the gift of American citizenship was bestowed on them. Could the "loyal minority" now bring their wives and families from China? Yes, said America, but only 105 per year. Those with wives were royalty, and the children born to those families walked the streets of Chinatown like princes and princesses among the aging kings of a generation made impotent by law. Old Chinese men patted the children's heads, gave them candy, bought them toys, prodded them to eat, told them stories, and put *lay shee* in their hands, because giving money to the next generation would bring both of them good luck.

Every one of those men knew Wood as "Hong Mak's number two son." If an old man, even a stranger, waved him over on the street, he always went, not so much for the gift he would receive, but because his father had told him that he represented the family and should always be respectful of his elders. He thanked each man for his gift and called him *ah bok*, uncle. The uncles had herbal cures for every one of the boys' illnesses. Sometimes a man they didn't know would stoop down and tie their shoes, pick up a lost mitten, find a quarter hidden behind their ear.

Years later, the boys would hear stories about the old men's lives in America, told over the clatter of mah-jongg tiles or sitting at the back table of a restaurant, where the kitchen help ate.

"Hey, kit, dat train from Oatlan' to Reno go ober the Sierra Nevada mountains in Californ'. We Chinese builded dat trains. No boolsheet! You read about da gold spike in school, huh?" Now set the history books straight, they said. They told the boys to ride the train to Reno someday. The owner of the restaurant gave them each a silver dollar to play on a lucky number.

When Wood and his brothers joined the army, they were war heroes to these old men even before they marched out of boot camp or stepped off American shores. There were other, bitter old men who would argue with Wood's father because they couldn't understand why the boys would go and defend the country that had kept them out and made pariahs of them in their youth. Theodore died in Germany. Wood's entire division was packed and ready to ship out to the Battle of the Bulge when his name and two others were called to fall out. They were transferred to the Army Corps of Engineers and sent back to college to finish their engineering degrees. But the war ended before Wood completed his degree and before Abraham got out of boot camp.

Raymond suspected it was easier being Chinese American when his father was his age. After World War II, Congress had repealed the Chinese Exclusion Act, finally allowing Chinese to become naturalized citizens. They had proven their loyalty in the war, fighting the Japanese. They had proven they were not Communists by marching in the streets of Chinatown waving the Nationalist Chinese flag of Taiwan, a tiny island nation most of Chinatown had never been to. When Wood got out of college and out of the army, he could be an engineer, unlike the Chinese engineers he knew, who worked in Chinatown restaurants before the war. There was no longer any second-class citizenship in America. The loyal were being rewarded.

A man who had been a prince of Chinatown could now become a prince of the city. A paycheck, a car—a Cadillac no less, parked off Broadway, by a stage door—a pinch bottle of Haig & Haig in hand. They knew him, they expected him, Wood flashed the bottle, some cash, they opened the stage door, there was a pat on the back, a couple of white gals from the chorus said "Hi, *Woody*" and "Gimme a ride in your new Cadillac" on their way to rehearsal, down a hallway someone said, "The gang's all here, Wood." There was good luck in the air. Wood understood every wink, every OK sign, every expression that came down the pike. They needed his presence. He belonged. He pulled a chair up to the table, set the pinch bottle next to the glasses, and said, "Deal me in."

Raymond's father was built like Edward G. Robinson, short, compact, and powerful. Even though Wood wasn't born in China and had never been there, he had inherited a traditional sense of what it meant to be Chinese, as if a generation's separation from the homeland had intensified and magnified the will of his parents to make him learn traditional Chinese behavior. By the next generation, all that survived was respect for family, getting a good education, getting a good job, writing thank you cards for gifts, and knowing what to do at funerals.

Once Raymond had moved back to the Bay Area, settled into a good job, and moved into a nice neighborhood, his father began reminding him of his duty to family—that is, to have children, to keep the family name alive. He instituted a kind of Edward G. Robinson silent disapproving pall over dinner.

"You're kind of quiet tonight, Dad. Are you feeling OK?"

His father finished sucking on the chicken feet, without looking up. Raymond realized he had sounded too perky, too patronizing. He hated *perky* and had no idea where that tone came from. He put his chopsticks down.

Wood raised his chopsticks to eye level and pointed them at Raymond, right between the eyes. "You are your mother's only son."

Raymond thought: *This is a good beginning because it allows me to* know that (1) I'm not his son and (2) the next statement is going to invoke major guilt because it will involve the failure to honor my dead mother.

"She's Chinese from China." The tense was wrong, because his mother was dead, but guilt kept the spirit present and made the memory immediate.

"Family means more to her than anything. She depends on you to keep the family alive." Wood lowered his chopsticks. The tense would shift now.

Wood picked up his teacup and sipped. "I'm happy your mother wasn't around to see you get divorced. I know things don't always work out, but in our generation you grit your teeth and bear it."

It was one of Helen's expressions, a slight misstep with American figures of speech. It drowned all Raymond's will to fight.

"What do you want me to do, Dad? I'm not getting back together with Darleen."

Wood shook his head and made a guttural Edward G. Robinson sound. He reminded Raymond of the importance of family and his responsibility, as an only son, to think about more than himself. It was difficult for Wood to talk like this, because he had always left those duties to Helen. He stopped many times during his lecture, trying to recall her exact words. As painful as he knew it was for his father to think about her, and familiar as the speech was, Raymond allowed Wood to talk. If he agreed too quickly, it would seem as though he were trying to dismiss the importance of his father's speech. *Follow in my footsteps and make the same sacrifices* was what he heard.

When Wood had finished, he sat back in his chair, in his undershirt and boxer shorts, and avoided looking at Raymond. It was not because he thought his son was a failure, but rather because Raymond reminded him too much of Helen. From the moment of his birth, everyone had said Raymond looked exactly like his mother, especially in the features everyone pointed to: "It's in the

eyes and the nose." Since Helen's death the comparisons had resumed.

"You're thirty-seven, Raymond," his father added, as he took the
dishes into the kitchen. "You don't have that much time." Then he
removed his jade wedding ring and started to fill the sink.

TWO NIGHTS AFTER Raymond's mother's funeral, his father had
interrupted the silence between them.

"I need you to sleep in the bed with me," he said without any
real sadness or self-pity. "There's too much space there." It was the
bravest thing his father had ever done.

They couldn't talk about depression, or sadness, or pain, or
grief, or any other unspoken and undefinable emptiness that invaded their lives and occupied the space between father and son,
man and boy. Each one had shared a private life—a wife, a mother.
Each tragedy from then on would have her name on it. In their soli-
tary moments, they would know how to label pain and sadness
without speaking, without naming the names out loud. Neither father nor son ever uttered the words "What are you thinking?" To
think out loud, to name the hurt, would push them into self-pity
and away from healing. When one spoke, the other responded with
silence. Silence was a bond, an understanding. Silence was love.

In the darkened bedroom, Raymond had lain still beside his father, listening to him talk in a way he couldn't talk face-to-face in a
lighted room.

"You know, when your mother was a young girl, a Chinese fortune-teller told her she would die before she was forty-two. She
never told you."

His father's voice and breath seem to have a darkness all their
own. *My mother's pillow,* Raymond thought. *My father's voice.* Wood
seemed to speak to Raymond as if he were practicing to speak to
him.

"Nothing the fortune-teller told her about when she would marry, or when her wealth would come, ever came true. So it was silly, she thought. She must have thought that. She died within three days of the date. I don't know how much she believed in fortune-tellers; she was born there, in China, we weren't. I don't know if she thought about it in the hospital. Maybe she knew. Maybe the knowledge made her give up. I don't know. Maybe she knew. Maybe the fortune-teller didn't matter."

I don't know. Maybe she knew. Maybe the fortune-teller didn't matter. Raymond repeated each word to himself as if he had been told to memorize them, as if all conversations were meant to be like that from then on.

Raymond's father knew that Chinese people believed a grave had to be situated so as to mold spiritual influences carried in wind and water, *feng shui.* He had gone to the library and learned these things and set about honoring them and restoring order to his world. He read that wherever a person goes, she takes with her the universal harmony of her village. Was the universal harmony constructed within the nine ancestral plots of land surrounding a common well? The five elements, Eight Immortals, Eight Diagrams, Three Great Beings, the twelve animals of the Chinese zodiac, Three Pure Ones, Ten Celestial Stems, Four Heavenly Kings, or the six breaths of nature? In the end, Wood could only identify with Kwan Yin, the Goddess of Mercy, who provides relief from pain and suffering and protects children.

He wasn't sure what exactly led him to choose a particular hillside from the cemetery map for Helen's grave, but when he reached the site, all the graves around him bore the names of Chinese. His doubts about bad omens were dispelled.

A breeze lifted the scent of dried spices at his feet, even though there were no plants growing in the manicured lawn near him. He touched the grass, and when he pulled his hand away, the palm of his hand smelled as if he had crumpled laurel leaves there and pinched wild mint under his nose. In his dry mouth, his tongue quivered at the scent of wildflowers. He thought he saw a peacock just at the crest of the hillside, its colors shed across the hillside. In the distance, San Francisco Bay shimmered in the haze of the afternoon.

He closed his eyes. The water pushed closer, until it nearly touched his feet. He saw his reflection there, and a whole world mirrored. But it wasn't his.

"I don't know. It's OK now," he said out of the dark next to Raymond, in answer to an unspoken question.

I don't know became embedded in Raymond's tongue. Whatever he didn't know about his future, he could find in his father's voice.

Raymond began to acquire his father's taste in food, food he had never liked before, as if he were occupying not the space beside his father but the same space. Bitter melon, artichokes, pickled pig's feet, *hom yu*, salted duck eggs. They shared the eyeballs and cheeks of steamed fish, sucked bone marrow, ground gristle and tendons between their teeth. He mimicked his father's handwriting. They sat and read the newspaper together and listened to news radio. Later, Raymond ordered his first drink in a bar by simply repeating what he had heard his father say. "Scotch, rocks." The liquor burned his father's words deeper into his tongue. He ate a crab and mixed the yellow meat inside the body cavity with *ng gah pay*. He lived his life as a series of symbolic gestures.

This imitation, Raymond knew, made his father feel safe; safe from blame, from terror, from what ifs, from guilt, from chaos. It was hard for Raymond to see his father going through his life as if he were the symbol of fatherhood rather than the father himself. In the Chinese world, being the first son gave one a sense of place, of belonging, of leading the family. Raymond's father gave him his place in the family by not telling him, by not asking, by not saying what was in his heart. It was the manly way of doing things. This was how Raymond became a man.

Five nights later, Raymond's father had sent him back to his own bed. He let his son go. "Why does life have to be so hard?" he asked Raymond. *I don't know. It's OK now.*

Day separated from night. By day Raymond lived his father's life, and by night he was returned to his mother. He knew no other death except hers. Their common lives became separate dreams. As an infant in an ancestral village where Raymond had never been, he was strapped to a woman's back, his head resting between her shoulders as she moved about the house, working, leaning, standing, walking through rooms, past windows where the sunlight flickered inside his closed eyelids. His dream was so real, he dreamed himself remembering all this: He heard the deep resonating vibrations through his mother's back as she spoke and labored in the fields. He heard his mother walking through shallow water, then felt her right shoulder dip down, then her left shoulder, his small arms and tiny hands clutching pieces of her clothing while he slept. A golden ash fell on the village and clumped into fist-sized chunks of gold. The rice the women had been picking turned to gold. His mother clasped her hands above her head in triumph. Each of the women carried Raymond in her arms and nuzzled him as if he had brought this gold.

Helen's death made Raymond more her son. Raymond's father began to speak of his wife as "your mother" or "Raymond's mother." Father and son held her in their memories as if they were the same man.

The first son in a Chinese family has certain duties to family as well as to himself, and over time the performance of these filial obligations is a test of patience and tolerance against personal ambition. Gradually, over the months and years following the death of his mother, Raymond was freed from living a life bound to his family. Was he freed by his father? He wasn't sure. His father had never dealt with him by invoking guilt or remorse. *You must do this for your mother. For your mother's memory.* Once in a while his father would say to him, "Be a good boy," in a tone of voice that hinted he no longer knew how old Raymond was.

Three years after the death of his mother, Raymond had left for college. He didn't have to be a doctor or a lawyer or an engineer or a dentist, like some of his Chinese classmates, who bore the burden of following in a father's footsteps, or being the first to go to college, to work hard, get good grades, be something their parents wanted them to be. Be a symbol. Be a good boy. Be a good son. Raymond never lived at home again.

What had he taken with him?

3 eye contact

WHEN RAYMOND STEPPED THROUGH THE FRONT DOOR, Aurora Crane wondered when he would notice they were the only two Asians at the party. She tried to avoid him, but failed. She touched him accidentally several times. They watched each other furtively from across the room.

Aurora had arrived first. They were *her* friends, *her* office mates, and it was *their* party. Raymond Ding was only a guest of her boss, the host of the office party, who had announced earlier in the evening that he had invited a visitor from out of town at the last minute, a friend of a friend, who was in D.C. for only a few days attending a conference. He wasn't in the newspaper business. With dread, Aurora realized that her boss would make a special point of introducing him to her, and that one by one her loyal friends would betray her and pair her with their Asian guest. There was no real covert activity, no setup, no blind date, no surprise dinner companion who happened to be seated next to her. She was not at home, meeting not so coincidentally her mother's idea of a "nice Japanese boy." She had a boyfriend—unfortunately in another city and not Asian—whom none of the loyal had met, although, to add to the misfortune, some of them knew she had moved away to define a future without him. It was all very complex in her mind, but simple in theirs. They would probably introduce her to the boss's guest several times during the evening. It would make sense to them.

She wondered how long it would take him to make eye contact. She hoped to God he wasn't an insecure Asian male who would talk only to her. She hoped to God he wouldn't see her as every Asian boy's perfect woman—just Asian enough to bring home to Mother while maintaining the white-girl fantasy. This was somewhat complex indeed, certainly more complex than the movie *Love Is a Many Splendored Thing*. If Aurora Crane was a Eurasian Jennifer Jones, was the Asian boy William Holden? He'd like to think so.

When he eventually got around to asking "What are you?" would he be different from any other obnoxious bore? Or would he simply be overly curious but too polite to ask? There would be that slow realization creeping over his face, the ponderings and machinations that nestled in the eyes, the slight squint, as if squinting could detect racial ancestry. He would ask finally, when she noticed he was no longer listening to her and merely watching her talk, all the while trying to decipher and calibrate the skin tone, the shape of the eyes, the color of the hair.

The truly devious and ignorant always asked where she was from. A city in Minnesota was not the answer they were looking for. Where are your parents from? Also from Minnesota and California was not the answer either. Sometimes she would return the favor and ask where the interrogator's parents were from, because, ha ha, everyone knew that nearly everyone in Washington, D.C., was from somewhere else. The truly inept (who were sometimes failed aspirants to be truly devious and ignorant) would blurt, "What nationality are you?" *American like my parents.* "What are you—you know, what race?" Was ethnicity so hard a word to use? "Oh, how wonderful to be Japanese and Irish! You're so pretty." At which point some D.C. matron would exclaim to her friend, "Miriam, don't you think she's pretty? That complexion!"

Sometimes they'd reach out and touch her skin without asking.

"Don't you think he's pretty?" Annie, one of her betrayers, nudged Aurora. "Maybe he's a Japanese businessman in town to argue import duties and the trade deficits. But then he's kind of tall."

Aurora, without looking at the visitor from the Orient, replied, "His suit is the wrong color. Eurotrash big shoulder pads, olive brown not Brooks Brothers American-cut charcoal gray. Hand-painted retro tie. West Hollywood is about as far east as this guy goes."

Asian people could tell she was part Asian; perhaps not part Japanese, but something. They knew at first eye contact. This eye contact thing between Asian men and Asian women was where the war began.

Aurora knew the battle well.

An Asian woman and an Asian man are the only two people on opposite sides of an intersection, waiting to cross the street. First there's usually one momentary point of eye contact to register race. He looks to see if he knows you or your relatives. If he doesn't, the competition begins. The men always weaken first. They look at the traffic, check the lights, check the wristwatch, then walk, never making eye contact again. At the critical point when eye contact should occur between the only two people on the street caught between the boundaries of a crosswalk, the men chicken out and check the time again or run as if they are late.

Just once Aurora would like to shock one of these boys and say, "Hey, home, what it is?" Whenever she was on the street with her black coworker Leon Dupree and heard him say that to another black man, she would ask if he knew the man. The fact that he never did made her wonder why it wasn't ever possible between

two Asians. Was it distrust? Was it historical animosity? Was it because Japan invaded China and Korea? Mao versus Chiang Kai-
shek? Chinatown versus Japantown? Fourth-generation Chinese
American versus fresh off the boat?

The exotic visitor from the East didn't have any Polo trade-
marks on his clothes, so Aurora ruled out Korean and decided he
was Chinese. She searched for the most typically Chinese feature
about him, but couldn't find the usual landmarks: cheap haircut
with greasy bangs falling across the eyebrows, squarish gold-
rimmed glasses, askew because there's no bridge to hold them up,
baggy-butt polyester pants, a shirt tucked in way too tight, perhaps a slab of jade on a thick twenty-four-karat gold chain around
his neck. He had none of the above but had a gift for the host and
hostess in a plastic shopping bag. *Please, please,* Aurora thought, *let
it be oranges!* Oh, it would be so Chinese to bring oranges. And, of
course, the plastic shopping bag—Chinese Samsonite. He was
made.

She knew she was being cruel. She had to be cruel in order to
steel herself for the impending introductions. Why she needed to
be cruel she wasn't sure, but she found herself looking for and analyzing the most un-Asian features about him. OK, the clothes
were certainly Beverly Hills or West Hollywood, all natural fiber,
beautiful colors. No man dressed like that in D.C., which was a
lawyers' dark-gray or navy-blue and red-tie town, no exceptions.
Maybe on Saturdays, for a walk on the wild side, khaki Dockers
and a polo shirt. She doubted if Asian American men in West
Hollywood dressed like him. That gave her a clue. OK, he was tall,
nearly six feet, which always gave Asian men the attitude that they
were tall enough to flirt with white women eye-to-eye and not have
to resort to either dominance or the cleverness of their shorter
counterparts with the Napoleon complex.

"Isn't he pretty, Ro?" Annie repeated.

"He's obviously got some Wonder Bread squeeze at home who dresses him."

"Well, there's one you don't have to make over," Annie said. "We deserve once in a while to find one who's already been made over—cute clothes, contact lenses, decent haircut, nice shoes—by some other woman. Jeez, the work we put into some of these guys, then they leave us because they're so presentable and depolyesterized."

Aurora was reloading another salvo, about a Chinaman shopping in Los Angeles on Rodeo Drive in a four-wheel-drive Range Rover with a golden retriever, when Annie said what she always said about Aurora's analysis of men. "Yeah, yeah, I know. We weren't born cynical, we were made cynical."

Aurora looked away when she saw her boss leading the Chinaman by the arm to the front of the room, where she was sitting. But instead of the introduction she feared, her boss announced, "Everybody, this is Raymond Ding from San Francisco, a friend of a good friend. Raymond is the assistant director of Minority Affairs at Jack London College in Oakland." Turning to Ding, her boss continued, "I'll let everybody introduce themselves. Watch out what you say on the record, Ray; they all work at the *Washington Post*." That was it.

Raymond surveyed the room and nodded hello to the group, without doing a double take on Aurora. Those closest to him began a discussion of San Francisco, out of which Aurora caught snatches of conversation about earthquakes and Italian food.

Maybe he thought he was too good for her. Aurora didn't know if she was relieved or disappointed. She was willing to give him a chance.

Later, through some miscalculation on both their parts, they ended up at the food table together, each entering the dining room by a different door. She handed him a plate by the buffet. They spoke briefly about the food and exited through the same separate doors. Upon reentering the living room, they noticed that their seats had been taken by others. A piano bench large enough for two remained. From across the room, he made eye contact, didn't look away, and motioned for her to share the seat.

Brave Chinese boy, she thought.

"Do you play?" he asked, pointing with his dinner plate to the piano. He wished those weren't his first words to her. Prop-dependent, boring, unoriginal. Raymond suddenly felt like the stereotypical interloper who sidles up to an attractive woman at a piano bar. *Do you come here often?* would complete the scenario.

Her answer was a simple and truthful "No." But the intonation in her "no" closed doors, broke hearts, and melted romantic inscriptions on sterling silver keepsake lockets with acid.

He said, "Food looks good." Prop-dependent, boring, unoriginal again. Should he say something funny now, like "My, how your eyes slant in this rich light. Hey, it's tough to get that *yin/yang* thing just right. How about those war brides, huh?"

"Are you a reporter at the *Post*?" That was the best he could do.

"Photographer's assistant."

Aurora snapped a carrot stick in her mouth. Perhaps, she thought, she should speak a little to the Oriental at hand just in case people were watching. "Was it Ray or Raymond?"

"Raymond is fine, but go easy on the Ding jokes."

"Aurora Crane."

Raymond smiled. He was being witty and clever in his mind. He knew without asking that her parents had named her Aurora because of the aurora borealis—a child of many colors. Perhaps her girlhood friends teased her and called her "A.B." for short. She was looking away from him, bracing herself for questions about her name, but Raymond posed them to her silently and smiled to himself at the answers. He wanted to say something about her hair, which was cut in an unusual asymmetric fashion—short on one side, angled on the other, with the angle tapering down to a chiseled point at her jawline. Her bangs were cut straight across, with the exception of an angled notch over one eye. He wanted to ask if that notch in her hair was where she placed her camera, but he knew she wouldn't think it was funny. He wanted to say he liked it, but thought he would sound patronizing because it was obvious that Aurora was younger than he by ten or twelve years. To non-Asians she would appear perhaps as much as twenty years younger. He hoped it wasn't that much of a difference. He didn't know why this mattered to him, except that they seemed to be the only two Asians at the party. He tried not to stare at her hair, or her smooth skin, or her greenish-hazel eyes, or her long, thin legs which stretched farther from the piano bench than his own legs even though he was perhaps four inches taller.

In an attempt to look elsewhere, he looked down at the plate of food she held in one hand. Aurora tugged at the hem of her short black skirt with her free hand. *Looks like a model, eats like one*, Raymond thought. The conversation, or the lack of it, was going badly. Perhaps she thought she was too good for him. Perhaps her boyfriend was at the party. Raymond scanned the room and tried to pick out which white guy was hers.

Back-to-back, they entered conversations on opposing sides of the room. At first they spoke at the same time, each conversation drowning out the other. The piano bench became a demilitarized zone in which all sensory contact between the two of them was prohibited. But each time she laughed she leaned back, touching, no, grazing him slightly. And each time the feeling lingered, as if they were holding a flower petal between them without bruising it, or a potato chip. The touching worked its way into their conversations, as they paused to eavesdrop on each other while feigning to pay attention to what was being said to them. It was a way of flirting. A simple touch from one would cause the other to stutter and lose a train of thought. While talking to Annie, Aurora overheard Raymond say he had been divorced for two years. While talking to Aurora's boss, Raymond overheard Annie and Aurora talking about the lack of interesting men in D.C. They would need this information later in order to gauge and measure the ground on which they would talk when the time came.

The "six breaths of nature" moved between them: wind, rain, darkness, light, *yin*, and *yang*. The perfect blend of each breath of nature settled the heart, mind, and body. Actually, neither of them paid much attention to the fact that it had been raining for days, it was dark, a bright piano lamp was glaring in their eyes as they spoke, and they were situated antagonistically back-to-back rather than allowing the complementary *yin*, which is dark and feminine, and *yang*, which is light and masculine, to find a place between them. But then that was just so much Orientalism under the rug.

He wanted to begin again. *Can I get you some more dip? Would you like to meet me for breakfast? What's your favorite monument? Have you read Edward Said's Orientalism?* He prepared for a new beginning, knowing that the conversation would eventually turn to include the two of them again. The longer the delay, the later the party went, the more impossible to get over this Asian thing between them. Solve the dilemma, get the facts about each other's preference for lovers not of their own race. *Nothing personal, you know. It's an individual thing, that love thing. We can get on with it, maybe even be friends, double date to prove how comfortable we are with voicing our racial preference to each other honestly and forthrightly. How adult of us; how politically correct.*

Was she part Korean or Japanese? he wondered. Or maybe he was altogether wrong and she was native Alaskan or Indian or Latino. What a relief that would be.

Raymond told her in his mind, with his back turned to her, "Let's say we've just arrived here in America from a foreign country—you from Korea, Ceylon, or the Forbidden City, me from New Jersey. I say to you at the supermarket checkout line where we meet, 'Hi, how are you?' in heavily accented English. You, having just learned about standing in the express lines, look down and say, in Korean, 'You have two too many items.' I give you my salami and oatmeal cookies because you only have four items. You buy them and leave.

"The next time I see you, you're taking English and prenursing classes at Seattle Central Community College. In the school cafeteria, I say, 'Hey, babe, how are you? What's your major?' You buy green Jell-O and leave.

"The next time I see you, you're getting an M.B.A. from Kansas and dating a Jayhawk, a six-ten power forward, full scholarship. He's no walk-on. You're his tutor. I see you in the library. I ask, 'Would you like to read my *Wall Street Journal?*' You put down your copy of *Der Spiegel* and glare at me. I say, 'I'm majoring in social work.'

"The next time I see you, you're at a dude ranch in Arizona, wearing cowboy boots with your jade. I resist calling you Slim.

"The next time I see you, you're buying leopard-print tights at Bloomingdale's. You're wearing a black suede dress with fringe. You've changed your name from something with too many syllables to Connie. 'How about some espresso, Connie?' I ask. You look down at the women's socks in my hands and I explain, 'I buy women's socks because I have small feet.'

"The next time I see you, you're trading in your Toyota and buying a four-wheel-drive Ford Bronco equipped with monster mudder tires and a chrome brush guard. Safest car in America. You'll never get in it with that skirt, I think. 'What's she got under the hood?' I ask. You peel out in reverse.

"The next time I see you, you're anchoring the news on television. 'How's the weather and what's the score?' I ask."

◆ ◆ ◆

RAYMOND WANTED TO SPEAK TO AURORA, but he couldn't. She looked too young, and at his age and divorced, it would be obvious what he wanted. He felt ashamed, guilty, and defensive. He worried that if they spoke, everyone seated around the room would eavesdrop and smile knowingly. They were, after all, the only two Asians in the room. The minutes ticked away. Raymond's bravery returned, then slipped away again as he envisioned himself as a Moonie with a pincushion haircut and a topknot, trying to give Aurora a flower.

He felt her rise from the piano bench, and when he finally turned to speak, she had gathered some empty plates to take to the kitchen. When she returned, someone else had taken her place on the piano bench. Their eyes met. He wanted her to come and sit on his lap or sit on the floor beside him with her arm draped casually across his leg, drink wine from the same glass, laugh at his jokes, squeeze his arm knowingly when it was time to leave. Eye contact, then it was gone.

He stood up from the bench because there wasn't a place for her to sit, made the same motion he had made when they first shared the bench. She shook her head and pointed at him, then at the kitchen. *Follow me.*

In the kitchen, they spoke for nearly an hour. No one interrupted them, because they were the only two Asians at the party. It was natural and meant to be. There was an occasional "Oh, I'm glad you two have met." He guarded against further cleverness and withheld any more prop-dependent, glib comments, and she found out he was actually a little shy. He did not squint to determine her ethnicity. She did not leave him guessing. Their conversation was complementary. She offered information, and he filled in the blanks without asking embarrassing questions. "I'd like to study Japanese at a language school in Kyoto," she told him. He asked if her mother was *issei* or *nisei*. She replied that her mother was *nisei*

and had met her Irish American father while selling him vegetables
from the family farm.

Aurora did not have to explain herself or her identity. Twice she
reached out and pulled him toward her to keep him from backing
into someone carrying a tray of food. When the danger passed each
time, he retreated a step. Perhaps he should have memorized Sun
Tzu's *The Art of War.*

In just this hour of talk, Raymond inferred that Aurora was not
the kind of woman who would place stuffed animals in her car,
buy Tupperware, or wear a dress with a zipper from the neckline to
the hemline.

Two days later, this was how she made him kiss her: He was
leaning against a column at the top of the stairs on the portico of
the Lincoln Memorial. She walked toward him, saying something
he couldn't hear, and leaned next to him, covering his arm with
her back. She nestled. He put his arm around her waist. Later, she
would deny this version of history, claiming her eyesight wasn't
that good and she had simply misjudged how close she was to him.
But she did not move away. They kissed at the top of the stairs of
the Lincoln Memorial, at lunchtime, in full view of schoolchildren
on a field trip from North Carolina. Raymond suddenly felt too con-
spicuously Chinese. Aurora held him close, and he kissed her on
her neck just under her left ear, which was exactly the right thing to
do. She did not breathe until she whispered in his ear, "Public and
demonstrative Asian love. A rare sight."

One of the little southern white children asked the teacher, "Are
they making a movie?"

Two years later, in San Francisco, they were packing their separate things and parting.

4 open curtains

RAYMOND WATCHED AURORA WALK ACROSS THE ROOM
and sit on the floor in front of the dresser. She pulled open a
drawer and began to sort through it, separating her things from
his. Too much had been said and too many things left unsaid.
Raymond suppressed the urge to discuss their first kiss at the
Lincoln Memorial and the several weeks of separation that followed after Raymond returned to San Francisco.

In the space between them they had flirted, she had scolded, he
had reminisced about their delicate kiss, she had changed the subject, he had politely probed the boundaries of their uncertain yet intimate talk, and she had questioned his motives. With each answer,
Raymond discovered his voice had a power in her ear. And with
each answer he moved closer to her heart.

He told her on the phone a week after kissing her, "I miss you."

"Because of one kiss, Raymond?"

"Another kiss under the ear."

He hardly knew her, except for their talk at the party, except for
a kiss now stalled by distance. If he were there, he would know
what to do.

"What would you do if you were here?" she asked, and, without waiting, offered her own answer. "Would you take me on a *date*, Ding?"

"Maybe we're past the formal date period."

"We never had a date."

"The Lincoln Memorial."

"That wasn't a date. I met you there after work, and you go and kiss me."

"You wanted me to kiss you."

"I *wanted* it. Listen to you! That'll stand up in court, Bud."

"You know it's true."

"Cliché number two."

"What did you do today?" Raymond wondered if she would let him wimp out and change the subject.

"I got my first photo in the newspaper."

Relieved, Raymond pushed congratulations on her much too loudly.

"Yes, Raymond." Aurora sighed. "Years of training, months of hauling camera equipment around and setting up lights for other photographers, and then, when the newspaper is short-staffed, I get my chance and the editor sends me out on my own to do what? Take a photo of the President? Perhaps some visiting king? Stalk a bad-boy congressman? No, none of the above. I, Aurora Crane, hit the big time, hit the pages of print, with a photo of a pothole in front of the White House."

"Did you get photo credit? Send me one. Signed 'love and kisses.'"

"When are you coming back?"

"Do you want me to?"

Raymond found out later that Aurora did not say the word "yes" much. One simply knew when she agreed. "I wish I were there now," he said, searching for some detail, some familiarity in imagining her at home. He resisted asking what she was wearing.

"I'm in bed," Aurora said. "Say it again."

"I wish I were there." There was a silence on the line, then he heard her breathing change.

Raymond retreated. "What does your room look like?"

"It's a mess."

"Let me guess. The shoes are thrown in a jumbled mess on the closet floor, there are old magazines and newspapers on the floor, the mug from this morning sits on the nightstand, with a little cold coffee in the bottom, the bookshelf is too small for all your books, there are unframed photographs thumbtacked to the wall, none of the photographs are your own, there are sweatpants, jogging shoes, and a bra lying on the floor. You're wearing an extra-large Columbia University T-shirt in bed."

Aurora was silent.

"Aurora?"

"Where are you calling from?"

"Home."

"Did you talk to my roommate? You have a sister you're not telling me about? You left out the color of my panties."

"No. And no to the second question. I was being polite on the third. The panties on the floor have purple dots, and the ones you're wearing have Mickey Mouse on them."

"You're wrong; they're both on the floor."

"I guess this means we're past the formal date period." Raymond's breathing had changed too.

"I'm wet."

Without hesitation, he continued, "You are seated on top of your desk when I come into the room. Your legs are crossed. I walk up to you and put my hand under your knees and uncross your legs."

"What are you doing?"

"I'm doing the same thing you're doing."

"I didn't know forty-year-old Asian men masturbate."

She knew he was thirty-nine, but he let it go. "We can even use the other hand to calculate logarithms on our Hewlett-Packard calculators." Aurora didn't laugh. Her breathing sounded muffled, as if she had gone under the covers of her bed.

"The backs of your knees are moist as I hold them down on the desk. I slide my hands up the sides of your thighs, feeling the muscles tighten. I'm moving so slowly that you relax. Your legs part slightly. I can feel your breathing on my neck. I reach around your hips, up the fabric of your panties to the waistband."

"I have tights on."

"I reach for the waistband of your tights."

"You can't get to them from where you are."

"My fingers are feathers. You can barely feel them. But they can lift you, they can warm you, they have a tropical humidity of their own. Your tights melt away. Your panties are a warm breeze that comes up suddenly, then vanishes, exposing a humid scented moss. My feathers flutter and nestle on the mound. My tongue is an orchid petal."

"That's too pastoral, but I like the fluttering."

"I'm trying to be polite on our first seduction. More graphic, dear?"

"No."

"How about mythic and heroic?"

"Yes, try mythic."

Like the voice that narrates pro football documentaries, Raymond was mythic and heroic. "The pulsating and golden aura of my manhood rises majestically in the east and blocks the sun. It presses, advances, draws you quivering toward me. It beckons you to embark on a voyage on the surging waves of a melting earth, a field of erupting, heaving mountains pouring white-hot magma down down down to the crashing waves of the ocean pounding the burning sand of your desire. We are reborn. We are immortal. Come with me. Come."

"Your manhood blocks the sun?"

"Yes, child."

"How big is this golden aura of manhood?"

"How big do you want it to be?"

"Big as a cucumber."

"How about a pickle?"

"I'm hanging up."

LONG-DISTANCE PHONE SEX and making love with Aurora in person had turned out to be verbally the same seduction to her. A good lover must be articulate first and skillful and attentive second. She wanted him to think and be coordinated and skillful all at the same time. In Aurora's bedtime stories Raymond learned to flirt, be romantic, be seductive, and undress her all at once, making love to her in complete sentences and full paragraphs. She wanted to be the center of his fantasy when they were making love, but each time the details had to be different: different clothing, different order in which the clothing comes off, different circumstances, different locations. They were characters in a story that had only a beginning and a middle.

"DO YOU HAVE TO WATCH ME PACK, Raymond?" Aurora asked.

"If you don't want me to watch, then ask me to help you."

"Help me pack or stay?" Aurora pushed a box across the floor and tossed Raymond a roll of tape. "The men in the movies say, 'I want you gone before I return.'"

"This isn't the movies. I don't want you to leave."

Raymond placed the roll of tape on the floor. With her back to him, Aurora rested her head on an open drawer. Unable to explain his love, to describe his need for her, or to ask once again that she not leave, Raymond got to his feet and made a motion to go and leave Aurora to her packing.

Aurora wanted to say something. Raymond waited and leaned against the wall. Unable to form words, she stood and hugged him, pressing her weight against him and pinning him to the wall. She pulled his shirt out of his pants, pressed her face to his chest, and tried to smell him through the fabric of his shirt. *Will I remember this as the last time we make love?* She unbuckled his pants, let them slide to the floor around his ankles, and blocked his attempts to kick his shoes off and free his legs by placing her knee between them. She wanted him to be slightly hobbled and awkward.

She whispered in his ear, "What do you want to do to me?" She turned her back to Raymond and leaned against him. She reached behind her and tucked her fingers in the waistband of his under-pants and pushed them down. He lifted her skirt. She stood on his shoes so that she was taller and accepted the way he nestled his erection between her legs. She liked the feeling of him, hard against the crotch of her panties. He pressed his cock against the fabric, pretending to be frustrated by his inability to enter her. He covered her right hand with his own and placed it on the buttons of her blouse. He kissed her neck and, from over her shoulder, watched her unbutton her blouse. He kissed her under her ear. The fear that this was the last time kept Raymond silent for once.

THE SEX STORIES he had told Aurora were politely phrased and plotted to indulge her. He spoke slowly so that he never had to re-vise or edit them. Each story was meant to be erotic only to a certain point, then the fantasy wasn't allowed to interfere with the way they touched each other. In their stories they were never someone else. When Raymond entered her it was always just him; Aurora would demand it. The stories were erotic because the circumstances were plausible. They were stories that began with something Aurora said or felt or wanted. Each story drew on their common sense of humor, their tastes, their voices, their hearts. Aurora interrupted and posed questions, sometimes in her own voice and sometimes in Raymond's. She said the words "suck" and "pussy" and "fuck" deliberately, as if she were quoting Raymond, as if he had said them first, as if one could hear the quotes surrounding each word. Each question pursued Raymond's motives and each question could only be answered with yes. She liked to hear him say yes. Sometimes he stopped in midsentence as he searched for ways of speaking with his hands, but he kept talking, and it was Aurora who unbuttoned, unhooked, unsnapped, unzipped.

It's afternoon. Very hot. Very humid. We couldn't sleep last night. In our exhaustion we've fallen asleep fully clothed on our bed in a hotel room with enormous windows and billowing white curtains.

We're bathed by the sunlight filtering through the opaque curtains. We're only one floor above a noisy street. Each time the breeze separates the curtains, there's a view of other buildings across the street, of windows mirroring the reflection of our hotel.

Are we in a foreign country? I'm not sure. The noise from the street stirs you from your deep sleep.

My hand rests inside your loose blouse, cupping your breast. Before opening your eyes you can feel my thumb brush lightly against your nipple each time your breathing rises and falls. You push my hand away and the sweat pooled there is cooled by the breeze pushing through the curtains.

Is it a tire screech or a bottle shattering against the pavement that wakes you? You unbutton your blouse, but you're too tired to sit up and shed it from your damp back. Your skirt is twisted and gathered and folded in the sheets. Some of the fabric of the skirt is matted against your thighs where you've been sweating. It irritates your skin. You push your skirt off. You're not wearing underwear and worry about the curtains parting.

You're beginning to remember your dream. You're angry with me. Something you dreamed made you angry. I was with two women, and we were laughing at you and how you discovered my infidelity. You're angry now for being naked and vulnerable while I'm fully clothed and disloyal. Your heartbeat is pushed by your anger. Another bottle shatters on the street. You weren't dreaming, you say.

Your fear wakes me. You turn on your side and look into my brown eyes before I'm fully awake to see where I've been, to confirm my infidelity. Instead of seeing guilt and fear, you see a sleepy insouciance. Your anger changes to irritation at having been awakened with a rapid heartbeat. By the time your hand reaches across and feels my slow heartbeat, you are convinced of my innocence.

"A little boy, a woman's fear," you whisper. I can't hear you over the noise from the street. Other people are talking. We are in a foreign country.

I lift your hand from my chest and place your palm against my forehead. "It's hot." You feel my cheeks with the cool backside of your hand. When I lick my dry lips, you rest a fingertip on the tip of my tongue. I expect to taste the salt of my own sweat; instead I taste you. You push your finger down against my tongue. I take your hand from my mouth and place it back down there; our fingers intertwine, you push my finger inside you, pull my hand from you, brush the wetness against your clit. My finger is cradled by yours. You teach me each delicate stroke. "The curtains," you say. "People can see us." My tongue circles your nipple. "We are in a foreign country," I whisper.

AFTER RAYMOND AND AURORA MADE LOVE, she rested her head against his chest, listened to his rapid heartbeat, his deep breathing, felt his body heat. Aurora was always amused by his exhaustion, which she had thought at first was an exaggerated performance calculated to please her. She hadn't thought that men could be so consumed by orgasm, thought they were only consumed by the satisfaction of having completed a task that required coordination, timing, and unselfishness. *How was I?*

She thought that his heart beat more rapidly than anyone's she knew, like a small animal nearly frightened to death. When she had questioned his state of exhaustion, he would only say, "I'm old." Raymond was not a man of routine habits like those who eat the same breakfast morning after morning, but he was a man of routine habits after making love. He would place his right hand over his forehead, then drag it down over his eyes as if he were thinking about something he could not believe or could not remember. He did not move his hand from his eyes until his breathing slowed, as if reality had sunk in.

IN THE DAYS THAT PRECEDED THEIR PARTING, Aurora attempted to sort her things from the dresser, but Raymond was always there as a reminder of what once was, what she wanted, and what she wanted to be separated from. In their mutual silence each remembered a series of discussions, some heated arguments and others simply too tired and familiar.

The first few months with Raymond had been like being in a college ethnic studies class, as they compared notes about being Asian in America and her being biracial. Raymond spoke of the sixties and seventies and ideas like "self-determination" and "multiculturalism," which she had only heard in school and never from a lover. In the sixties, Negroes had become blacks, and Raymond had become "Asian American"—without a hyphen. Sometimes he lectured in bed about institutionalized racism.

For him it wasn't enough that she simply know which box to check on the affirmative action form. She needed to know the exact definitions of race and ethnicity, the history of the struggle, the symbols of institutionalized racism.

"What did your mother tell you about the camps?" Raymond asked.

"She was a little girl, Raymond. She said she didn't notice what the adults noticed. She remembered being able to play all day. She said it was dusty."

"Did she end up in the Midwest because of the War Relocation Authority's prohibition that families not settle in the western so-called military zone?"

"Why don't you ask her?"

"You're supposed to ask, Ro. That's the whole point." Raymond pointed at her, while turning in the bed to face her. "If you don't know what questions to ask, you lose your history; when you lose your history, you lose your sense of self."

"My uncle was in the army," Aurora said, as proof she knew something.

"Was he in the all-*nisei* 442nd Regimental Combat Team or the 100th?"

"I don't know, Raymond. He showed me a Nazi dagger once."

"Were any of your other uncles *no-no boys?*"

Because she couldn't remember what a *no-no boy* was, she simply shook her head.

Raymond continued anyway. "In some ways your mother's family was lucky, because the loyalty oath given in the camps ended long friendships, caused riots, divided families, and ended marriages."

Aurora, who knew all this information in a general way, listened patiently, but all she really wanted to know was how long Raymond's hair had been and what he had worn when he was at Berkeley.

At first they had joked about Raymond bringing her to San Francisco, as if it were the promised land for those confused about their identity. Raymond could only imagine what it was like to grow up in a household where one parent is Asian and the other is white. "It was really quite simple," Aurora had said. "My mother was my mother, and my father was my father." But Raymond thought it was more complex. He thought predominantly Asian San Francisco, with himself as her lover and mentor, could tip the ethnic balance. He thought his ancestry was a gift. Their union was never just love and desire and friendship to him.

Aurora wondered if the differences between them were strictly a matter of race. Sometimes she thought Raymond made too much of the whole issue. As a couple, they made visual sense. When she was with Raymond, people assumed she was Asian and didn't have to guess. It was the same with the city. She identified with it—was identified by it—in the same way that she was identified as Asian when she was with Raymond. But sometimes she found San Francisco too Asian. "Sometimes I miss having little white boys stare at me in the supermarket because I look different," she confided to her old friend Brenda, who had moved back to California after a stint in D.C., where she and Aurora had met. "Don't you?" And there were other times when she hadn't had to be Asian at all.

Raymond could not understand. He would only say, "I guess you haven't learned a thing. Don't you know in America skin color is your identity? This is a racist country. You can't be invisible." Yet sometimes she caught him telling people she was half Japanese before they even asked.

"Are we too insulated here in the Bay Area?" Aurora asked.

Aurora's younger sister, Julia, could pass for white. Unlike Aurora, she didn't look Asian, Hispanic, Italian, Native American, or Indeterminately Exotic. Her skin was much paler than Aurora's, and she had freckles. In college she dyed her brown hair blond and it didn't look odd. She thought about joining a sorority. Aurora was tall and thin, while Julia had what her father described as a "stocky and sturdy Japanese pearl diver peasant body." Her mother described her body as "athletic" and said her legs were shaped like *daikon*. She didn't need to wear shoulder pads, and she looked good in a bowling shirt. People asked if she was a swimmer.

She didn't hide the fact that she was half Japanese if someone asked. Usually no one asked. On survey forms she checked "Other" and filled in the blank. When she was young, adults often assumed that her mother was her nanny. She corrected them aggressively, in a voice much too loud and clear. Occasionally they would respond, "Well, you tell your mother that she's got a beautiful little girl." Norma would clap a hand over Julia's mouth and drag her off before she had a chance to retort.

Norma was used to it, but her daughters never got used to it. She would ask them to use their quieter, "Japanese voice," but they ignored her, and when she complained to Hank about their rudeness he just said he didn't intend to raise grin-and-bear-it kind of girls. He taught them auto parts shop talk and, by the time they were in high school, had them driving all over town in Aurora Auto Parts delivery trucks. It was common knowledge that "parts girls" had to be young and beautiful; that was how a store stayed in business. Sometimes they were the only women a mechanic or machinist saw during the working day. Aurora and Julia learned to dish out raunchy one-liners to the men who flirted with them. Norma despaired over their foul language, what she called "garage talk." Outspoken Julia was the favorite. Aurora was a little too beautiful, and her arrival could bring a forty-five-dollar-an-hour repair shop to a halt. When the men signed the receipts she handed them, they always wiped the grease from their hands on the shop rags first and signed their full names. Behind her back the mechanics called her Harvard, in appreciation of her class. Julia's receipts had thumb prints, scrawled initials, phone numbers. ("If you're writing that for me, you might as well put your wife's name too, so I'll know who I'm talking to when I call, you dog.") Her nickname was Bud, as in, "Hey, Bud, you want to grab a Bud after work?"

"You buying me a *whole* beer by yourself this time, or have you boys gone in on this together?"

"Hey, Bud, why don't you wear your cheerleader outfit for us to-morrow?"

"I'll be sure to tell your daughter that you asked when I see her in homeroom."

Julia probably could have been groomed to take over the business, but by the time she got out of college, conglomerate-owned discount auto parts stores were clearly the future. She became a medical technician and got a job in a pathology lab in Minneapolis. Along the way she also acquired a boyfriend, Miles Brown. Named after Miles Davis. End of that subject at the Crane household.

◆ ◆ ◆

"YOU KNOW that you're never seen as white," Raymond said.

"So why live that lie?"

"I'm not living a lie!"

"Well, maybe not a lie, but you can't pass as a white woman."

"Who's trying to pass?"

"Well, maybe not pass."

"What, then?"

"You are a beautiful and politically correct Asian American woman when it's convenient for you. Other times you let things pass without comment. Men think you're beautiful, and you're quick to point out that they're being racist when it affects your identity, but you're not being responsible at other times for the race. Each time you let something pass that's generally insulting or racist about Asian people and it isn't specifically directed at you, you're in a sense *passing* for white, or at least non-Asian."

"You don't think I have a conscience?"

"You have a conscience; it needs to be broadened." Raymond wanted to retract the word "broadened" just as he was saying it.

"Not everyone can be a professional affirmative action officer like you. I'm your lover, not a case history."

"Because you're part of my world, you have to understand the things that are important to me."

"Whatever happened to just having a woman understand the intricacies of major league baseball?" Aurora knew retreating to the trivial wasn't a good strategy to use, because it meant Raymond would press her even more. She tried to guess where he would go next with their conversation. If she had the energy, she would try complimenting him now: *You're a good lover.* From the trivial to the sexual would change the direction of the conversation, but Aurora knew Raymond was trying to be instructive. She hated his instructive tone. She hoped he wouldn't talk about the army. Aurora remembered how odd it had been when she first heard about Raymond's army experience, because she kept thinking how it had been so much easier for him to talk about his mother's death than about being in the army.

He had stood on the edge of the war, just as his father had stood at the edge of World War II. He had drawn a low draft lottery number and was plucked out of college when student deferments were canceled. He was inducted and, by a stroke of luck, was assigned to the Presidio in San Francisco, where he served as company clerk because he could type sixty words a minute. But a returning sergeant who had been wounded in combat had other plans for him. "Get that fuckin' gook out of my office," he had yelled. "I don't give a shit if he's a Chinaman—in 'Nam a gook is a gook. I ain't turnin' my back on him. If you don't move him now, I'm sending his ass to Vietnam." Amid a circus of delays, misunderstandings, accidents, and forgotten orders, Raymond was ordered to go to Vietnam. The sergeant told Raymond he was doing him a favor. "Wait till the gook bitches get a load of you, a gook brother with an American passport. Let freedom ring, Ding!"

The war came to him in secondhand stories from other soldiers at the Presidio. "They don't care what kind of fuckin' gook you are—if you want to stay alive there, don't be the enemy. When I look at you I see black hair and slanty eyes. Grow a beard. And don't go swimming. Do you understand? The Vietcong don't wear no uniform, and if you ain't wearin' yours no one is going to ponder shit over the smoke of a grenade blasting the yellow puke out of you. Your best buddy better be a black grunt, like your Siamese twin. Standing next to a black dude makes you the right kind of gook, unless the son of a bitch who's got you in his sights hates niggers. Ha ha ha!" End of basic training.

But his tour of duty to Vietnam was over before it began, when an army doctor, perhaps out of revenge for being newly drafted himself, discovered a flutter in Raymond's heartbeat; he called it a congenital murmur. Whether it was there or not, it was official, and the army discharged Raymond as if they were afraid he'd die of natural causes on them. Raymond never mentioned the few months he was in the army; only his father and the family knew. In later physicals there was no murmur.

Raymond knew he didn't have the right to own a part of the tragedy, would never know "what it was like." He had stood, paralyzed, on the fringe of the demonstrations that took place on campus, never raising his voice. He didn't believe his fellow students knew "what it was like" either. He believed in the cause of ending the war, but when he looked at the faces of the students, he couldn't substitute their young faces for those he had seen in the army, any more than he could substitute his own face for the face of the enemy.

Decades later, after the Vietnam Memorial had been built, Raymond would run his fingers over the names etched into the black granite and feel that he didn't know a single name of someone who had died in the war. All he could remember, all he could dredge up within him, was the fear he'd felt when the sergeant had called him a "gook." That, and the desire he'd brought back from his few months in the army to be anonymous in the world. There was a safety in being Asian American at home in America. *We work hard. We keep quiet. I am the model minority. Don't shoot me, I have a black friend. Bring them home. Firebase. Homebase.*

"I WANT TO BLAME YOU for whatever went wrong with our relationship. It would make more sense when I tell my friends that you were too old or that you hadn't gotten over your divorce. Me being not Asian enough or not culturally sensitive enough doesn't make for very interesting girl talk. It's part of your profession to help define a more equitable future, getting the affirmative action quotas right at the college and all. It's my job as a news photographer to simply record history. I can't change the photographs."

"I'm not talking about our jobs—"

"Sometimes you're a natural teacher, Raymond, and other times you're like all other men—full of bullshit. I know more about what you preach and talk about in the things you don't say than in the things you do say. You tell me you were in the army and were supposed to go to Vietnam but you were discharged when they found out about your heart murmur. You didn't come home with any combat wounds, but you did come home wounded from all the overt racism in the army and having to hear every day that the enemy were slopeheads, and gooks, and Chinks. Did you hate the enemy too? Did you hate the enemy for making you wear the same labels? It's not my generation, but I can see you brought the war home like the veterans who fought, only your battle scars didn't come in combat. You don't talk about Vietnam because it hurts. It made you more visible; I know that from what you don't say." Aurora couldn't believe that *she* had brought up Vietnam. Was she trying to hurt him?

"You don't say."

"Don't be glib." Aurora glared at him. "Is this the way we're supposed to talk, Raymond?"

"No."

"Now you're quiet because I said too much. Is the conversation broad enough? Sometimes, Raymond, I just wanted you to say that I'm the center of your life and that you love me. Why does the whole world around that center always have to be something called Asian America?"

"That should be obvious."

Raymond, too, wondered if the differences between them were strictly a matter of race. Had he been so adamant to "teach" her simply because he couldn't forget that Aurora was half white? Was he harboring some guilt for having a half-white girlfriend instead of displaying pride for having a half-Asian girlfriend? He argued with himself about race and gender, race and identity, being a flimsy excuse, a cover-up, a scapegoat for deeper problems between them. Under self-interrogation his answers sounded defensive. "What else is missing?" he wanted to ask her.

WITH THEIR SEPARATION PENDING, they stopped rehashing the arguments that had led to it. What was left was simply the differences between men and women, between two lovers.

"Let's have a different argument," Aurora said.

Raymond agreed.

"You're a man, I hate men."

"Yes, I agree: I am one."

"Men are scum."

"Yes."

"I have no life."

"You have me."

Raymond said something that he had said before, only this time Aurora was listening. "The disagreement between us is not the difference between men and women, but between sons and daughters."

"What's the difference?" Aurora began to look upset in that familiar way. She thought he was changing the subject in order to deflect an argument. When the subject turned to families, he had it all over her, because his was more Asian. How could she have let herself fall into that old trap?

There's no trap, Raymond wanted to tell her. He said, "What did your mother want to be?"

"She was my mother."

"No, what did she want to be? An artist, a ballet dancer? Did she ever want to be Myrna Loy?"

"What are you talking about? I don't know."

"The difference between us is in the way our mothers raised us. I was raised by a mother who raised me on extravagance and perfection. When my mother arrived from China, she took photography and painting. She was a Picassoesque self-portrait with baby. Everyone said I had her nose and eyes. My baby pictures were social statements, natural-light black-and-white photos heavy with shadow and bleakness, symbolizing man's alienation from society. A baby seated in a desolate corner of a room, framed against an immense blank wall. A baby's innocence measured against some

large impersonal machine of industry. The tender smooth skin of a
baby, a shard of glass, a broken gear. In between painting and photography, my mother went to the movies. In America she wanted to
be Nora Charles in *The Thin Man*. She bought me a wire-haired ter-
rier like Asta. Maybe she didn't want to be Nora Charles, but I know
she wanted her life to be like that—affluent, but more important
than affluence, she wanted to move through her daily life with the
same ease that Nora Charles moved through the daily routine of her
life. Things get done, people open doors, taxis are hailed, mysteries
are solved. It was her way of being an American. My father kept her
from naming me Nick."

"You know the sexiest thing about you?"

Aurora's trap. She told Raymond men were scum, then pushed
an idea toward him he could not resist. She never asked questions
that were soft and open-ended, like "What are you thinking,
honey?" She argued and made love with him by asking questions,
and both were forms of entrapment and seduction.

"I asked, 'Do you know the sexiest thing about you?'"

"Do you remember the first time we made love?"

Aurora looked up at Raymond in frustration.

"On the phone."

Her look changed to resignation.

"Why did you open yourself up like that? We hardly knew each
other."

"You're complaining?"

Raymond shook his head.

"I felt it would be fine. I told Brenda about it. She thought you
were a pervert. Don't worry, I told her the truth, how I started it, I
wanted it to happen. There was something about you being my first
Asian lover; there was a lot I didn't need to guard against, second-
guess, protect."

"I don't understand."

"You don't see it, Raymond?"

He shook his head again.

"You ever go into a Chinese or Japanese restaurant with a date who is white or black? Well, how do you feel? You're scrutinized and made to feel like the outsider. Your date doesn't feel any of this friction and tension. He feels like he's been taken inside; you're going to order the good stuff, maybe talk a little lingo with the waitress for his benefit. He might even throw in a little *arigato*, trying to get on your good side. There you are, eating, perhaps feeling the disapproval of the waitress, the busboy, all the while you're trying to figure out if your date is one of those guys who's got some kind of Asian-woman thing. And that 'thing' runs the gamut from asking you to teach him how to use chopsticks, to figuring he's going to get a shiatsu massage, to wanting his tea leaves read, to trying to find out if my vagina is slanted.

"You know why I've always kept my hair short, don't you? To screen out the white guys with the Nancy Kwan fetish. I've never been with any non-Asian man who hasn't at one time or another during our relationship tripped himself up and said something racist. They don't understand it when I say I'm not white. Their defense is that I'm half white.

"Hearing your voice on the phone, remembering how you kissed me on the neck, I felt free to leave myself unprotected, unguarded. The worst you could do was say something sexist. I could teach you to be less sexist and lower the toilet seat and all. As I talked with you, I realized you'd let me just be a woman, not make me be an Asian woman—which is, ironically, what Asian women say they want to be when they're with a non-Asian man. I knew you wouldn't make being an Asian woman part of the sexual fantasy—you know, 'Speak Japanese to me, baby, while I whack off.' That's why I wanted you." Aurora said all this without looking at Raymond.

"You make it sound so romantic."

"You're the only boyfriend I've ever had who uses the word 'romantic.' It *was* romantic, Raymond. Our fantasies were on the same plane. I thought you had the will and the desire to make me happy."

She suppressed the urge to tell him she would stay with him. "You didn't answer my question about the sexiest thing about you."

"We had simultaneous orgasms over the phone?"

"So you say." Aurora shot him a look of disapproval. "You didn't have to describe it."

"I was inspired."

"You're avoiding my question."

"Do you want me to guess?"

"Your patience with women. I've noticed it's how you flirt with women. You sit and listen. You actually want to be friends, and maybe several years down the road, something hits them and they want to go to bed with you. Women come up and kiss you, sometimes right in front of me."

"Friendly kisses—"

"That's the way you flirt. You walk into a room or a party or a dinner never expecting a kiss, nor do you look comfortable giving or receiving them. Keeping your distance is in itself a very flirtatious act."

Aurora felt stupid saying this. She knew that some of the women, closer to Raymond's age, kissed him in front of her only as a way of holding ground, of putting a stake through her youth and beauty. The women he worked with either had the politically correct talk, were born in Chinatown, went on pilgrimages, or had shared the political memory of the sixties and seventies with Raymond. When Aurora saw them at fund-raisers and office functions, they acted like jealous lovers instead of "sisters in the struggle." She understood their resentment toward her. Raymond's attraction to her confirmed a stereotype. There weren't many single men in their late thirties and early forties, and Raymond had done the very predictable thing of finding a younger woman. Raymond saw her as half Asian; they saw her as young and pretty. "So where did you meet Raymond?" seemed to be the only question they wanted to ask her. After a while, Aurora wanted to say that she had met Raymond at her high school when he came to recruit new minority students for the college, then one thing led to another. You know.

Aurora had noticed how women who greeted other men by stiffly accepting a kiss on the cheek, at most returning a peck, greeted Raymond with a kiss, sometimes on the lips, sometimes while he was in the midst of talking to someone else. Aurora suspected they liked to see Raymond's surprise and watch his insecurities rise to the surface. It was like having a certain power over him, and the more beautiful the woman, the more forward the kiss. Her best evidence was their own first kiss, with the exception that she had made him kiss her. And Raymond could be terribly flirtatious himself. Aurora had observed that he couldn't talk to a beautiful woman without trying to charm her. "You say you're just being friendly, but it's friendliness with intent. You should start a charm school. 'What's the harm in charm?' could be your motto." Aurora wanted to describe him as inscrutable, in the most well-meaning version of the word, the Sam Shepard-inscrutable-silent-attractive version of the word, but obviously she couldn't use that stereotypical word. She couldn't believe she had drifted from resentment to jealousy.

Raymond was going to say that perhaps the women just wanted to kiss someone Chinese, but he didn't.

Aurora continued. "Look at the way you make love. You want to talk and play at the same time. There's no rush. Most guys approach women like some lone dog, with the rest of the pack behind them barking encouragement. They measure their advances as victories and defeats. Why am I the one saying the dirty words? Where did you learn how to flirt like that? Are you conscious of it?"

"I must have learned it from my mother."

"Flirting and seduction?"

"No, patience." Raymond laughed. "I learned it by following my mother on shopping trips to San Francisco, to I. Magnin, City of Paris, Macy's. I remember her being very proud of the way the women clerks used to compliment me on my ability to stay interested in shopping for my mother's clothes. In the old days the department stores had huge, elegant dressing rooms, and I'd sit there and watch my mother try on clothes. The clerks thought it was so cute the way she asked my opinion. I'd sit there like some midget sugar daddy and say, 'I like it. I'll buy it for you.'"

Raymond surprised himself by his willingness to talk about his mother. Because she existed only in his memory, everything she had done or they had done together had symbolic meaning. He could tell the stories to Aurora but couldn't talk about the symbols. These symbols were no longer the cultural traditions that bordered a Chinese son's life of duty and obligation to mother and father. The symbolic markers were, for Raymond, suddenly finding himself close to the age when his mother had died and, because of this, realizing their lives were running parallel to each other. His life was free from the filial duties of a Chinese son but not from a hidden grief.

"Sometimes I think it's easier for you than me," Aurora said. "You're the loner. You're free to do whatever you want. Your mother is whatever you want her to be in your mind. Your father is content to start a new life and isn't dependent on you. Why am I struggling? Why don't I understand my father?" She paused. "Maybe because I'm a daughter."

"If you had been born the first son rather than the first of two daughters, would life have been different? Perhaps your mother's life would have been more extravagant. What are you afraid of?"

Aurora frowned. "We were arguing about us."

"We were not arguing. You said, 'Men are scum.' I agreed."

"Why do you always buy green onions when we go to the grocery store?"

"The last bunch is rotten." Raymond let Aurora retreat.

"It's rotten because we didn't eat it."

It was an inheritance. Raymond's mother always bought green onions, every trip to the market. She broke off and stole thumb-sized pieces of ginger from the Safeway. "It's not even enough to weigh," she told him. Aurora's inheritance was that she saved things like her mother did: useful things like the Styrofoam trays meat was packaged in, rubber bands, wire ties from plastic bags, plastic soup containers from the takeout, Ziploc bags. Letters. Raymond's mother never saved anything, never bought the economy size. What never changed between them was what they had inherited from their parents.

"Things have changed," Aurora said.

Raymond wanted to be saved from the way things change, from fear of change. He suddenly felt that he should quit before he was fired. He wanted to separate his things from Aurora's before she spoke again, before she was finished sorting her things from his. He didn't want to get caught showing her how much he was in love with her as she was preparing to leave.

I can be your friend, Raymond wanted to tell her.

Aurora pulled out another drawer and began to examine the contents. "It's ironic how your conceit involves other people in your life—the way it involves me. You're proud of your patience in my presence. You're proud of your shyness, which you say is confidence. You can be weak and vain about your image in my presence. Is that possible?" She went on as if she were talking to herself. "I think I've fallen in love with the image of you being alone, aloof, shy. You give people close to you their freedom to grow, and yet you don't allow this relationship to end. Trust the memory more than the thing itself. I don't want to hurt you."

Raymond couldn't speak. Each time she said she didn't want to hurt him, it hurt him. *Yes, I can be a friend. Yes, I can be a brother. I can help you get a job. I can fix your car. Men like me have tools.*

"What was the logic behind having both our underwear in the same drawer?" Aurora asked, then waved Raymond off as she remembered the punch line about intimate apparel. "Things have changed." Everything she had taken out of the drawer she put back. "We need to clean our house. There are things we need to throw away, but I can't throw anything away."

Aurora recognized the double meaning in what she had said and steeled herself against Raymond's self-pity, how he would want to say that he wished it were true. The silence was worse.

Raymond ignored the self-pity and tried to be funny. "Why do you save old copies of *People* and, of all things, *TV Guide?* Of what use is six-month-old news about shoulder pads, Calvin Klein, Nastassia Kinski, Lyle Lovett, and Arsenio Hall? If you need a halfway house and can't bear to throw the magazine away, tear out the articles you want to save, put them all in one box, save them for exactly one month, then throw them away.

"Throw away socks, T-shirts, underwear, tights, if any of the following are true: (one) there's no elastic left; (two) there are holes in—pick one—toes, butt, crotch, armpit, sleeves, heel; (three) you haven't worn them in five years; (four) you haven't worn them since high school; or (five) you've never worn them because they're too damn ugly.

"Throw away cosmetics or medicine if: (one) you're allergic to it; (two) you haven't used it in five years; (three) it's not the same color it once was; (four) you hate the color; (five) it belongs to your sister and you stole it from her; or (six) the bottle/box/ tube is empty."

"You make it sound so easy."

"Things of sentimental value are difficult to throw away. There are sacred items that can never be thrown away except in a fit of pique or despair, such as letters, photographs, corsages, teddy bears, ticket stubs, college sweatshirts, diaries. And yet the more you throw away in this category, the more it will feel as if your life is moving forward. It's like our Law of Interior Space Physics, which states that if we move the furniture in our home around, we will create movement in our lives."

This last part Aurora recited with him. They laughed. Then she reached into the underwear drawer and began to sort again. "Do you remember what I said to you when I thought you might try to seduce me after we kissed at the Lincoln Memorial?"

"Yes."

"Well?"

"You said, 'You're either genuinely nice or very very smart.'"

"Why didn't we sleep together that night?"

"It took me weeks to decide on an answer."

There were things Raymond couldn't say to Aurora now. He wanted to say, *Look at the thing you're throwing away. Remember the moment, the time, the person, the feeling, then throw it away. It will stay with you. There are things I can't bear to throw away, like everything I have that belonged to my mother. Yet everything that I've lost, the memory of that object, that thing, is burned in my memory. Somewhere in my moving years ago I lost a family album. I've memorized every photo in it.*

"You bought me a dress. I haven't worn it in months."

"Trust the memory more than the thing itself."

Aurora examined a pair of panties, then put them back in the drawer as if she were leaving them behind. "That's my expression; you stole it from me." She placed everything in the drawer again and pushed it back into the bureau. "I don't know who I am when I'm with you. I look at you and I think you're beautiful, but I don't see me anywhere in you. I'm not on the surface."

Raymond moved to speak but didn't have a defense against the truth, and she stopped him before he ended up in an awkward space between lying and insincerity. Aurora was afraid of what she had said. Even in separating from Raymond she appreciated the way he made their conversation specific to them, to who they were, and kept away from the clichés. She didn't want to sound like a whiny white yuppie couple mouthing things they'd heard on television or in a college psychology class about distance, about finding one's own space, about needs, about dysfunctional relationships.

"I'm not on the surface," she said again. "You look at some men and they have an aura about them that says how much they love their wife, their girlfriend. Or they wear their obligation on the outside; it says they have to run and bring the paycheck home, buy groceries, make sure there's air in the spare tire for their daughter's date." She tried to sound more specific but ended up drawing a picture neither of them wanted, nor were they capable of producing it between them. She saw Raymond trying to imagine himself in each of the examples. She wanted to say, *But not you, but not you.*

Aurora pushed herself further away from Raymond while at the same time stretching out her legs and resting her foot on his ankle. "Maybe it's my fault. I wanted my father to give me this too. I know my mother wanted him to publicly exhibit that he was a part of our lives: his Japanese wife, his two Eurasian daughters. But I don't think he really knew how. There were the three of us, and him. He never looked like he belonged to us and we never looked like we belonged to him. My father's an old navy man; he's got tattoos on his arms, for chrissakes. I remember he came to visit me when I was going to Columbia, and we were walking down the street on the Upper West Side. People were staring at us, my father with his Midwest plaid shirt, windbreaker advertising our auto parts store, his arm around my waist. He's still got his navy crew cut. I thought people were staring because he was so Midwest, but then I saw it in their eyes. I wasn't his daughter, I was a prostitute. They've seen me in the movies. The sailor and the pretty Asian girl. When I'm with you I'm safe from blame."

"Just because I'm Asian."

"That's part of it, and it's what I wanted. I wanted at least our identity together to influence me, to lead me, to make me feel like I belonged to you."

"Feminists—"

"Not in a way that'll have every Asian feminist up in arms, pointing her finger at me—"

"At me the misogynist or, at the very least, the domineering Asian man making a slave of you, the impressionable young girl."

"No one will ever accuse you of being a misogynist or domineering. Brenda once said you were a man who was taught how to be a man by a woman."

"Brenda said that? Brenda doesn't like Asian men."

"She thinks Asian men are sexy."

"I've never seen her with one."

"She doesn't want to go out with them; she just likes the way they look and the fact that they don't smell when they sweat. She sees all of you as sweet-smelling, mute Bruce Lees."

"How do you see me?"

"I was in love with the way we were a family. People saw us and it made sense to them."

"Except you're eleven years younger and look twenty years younger."

"That never bothered you. Why?"

He thought if he could keep Aurora talking, she might find her belief in him, in them, again. He tried to pick an argument, but he wasn't very good at it.

"So it's the age thing."

"It's not the age thing."

"It's the voice of experience thing."

"It's not the experience thing."

"I give too much advice."

"I ask you for advice."

"I'm Chinese and you're not."

"It's not racial."

"I'm a bad lover."

"You know the answer to that."

"I think your friends are young and silly."

"Some of them are."

"I patronize."

"You never patronize."

"I'm perfect."

"It's my fault, not yours."

"It's not your fault."

"I think I'm frightened by something."

"What is it, Aurora?"

They both knew. It was hard for Aurora to believe in her own safety, to feel protected. She wanted Raymond to protect her. Protect her from what? From what happens, from what ifs? No. She wanted to be as strong by herself as she was with Raymond. She wanted to have a son's sense of the world. She wanted her father to pass his power and authority to her as if she were an Asian son. She wanted people to witness King Lear handing the kingdom over to the loyal daughter. *Give me the pocket watch from Grandpa, turn over the business, pat me on the back when I follow you into the navy, live your life through me, your son, and grab me another beer, will ya?* The witnesses Aurora saw only heard her saying, "Hey, sailor." She couldn't see herself as an heir to anything.

Was Raymond the father who made sense of her identity? He was more than just her lover, she knew. It upset her that Raymond acknowledged he was not as strong without her. "I'm older," he had said more than once. "Maybe I know there are things I simply can't do anymore, can't prove anymore, or don't want anymore, or things I accept as they are." He talked about himself like a car: "As is, no warranty."

AURORA WAS AFRAID that she would never forget the way she and Raymond made love.

"How can you be afraid of that?" Raymond asked. "Is that something you want to forget?"

"This isn't the argument we're supposed to have."

"What?"

"You're deflecting the real reason we're breaking up."

"We've had that argument too many times."

"You're right," Aurora said, as if she could close all further conversation about their history.

In the end, Raymond moved and Aurora stayed in the apartment because he could not bear to see her leave.

Aurora knew that Raymond imagined fear and loss far greater than what life had proven as real fear and real loss. He couldn't live in the apartment that held the memory of the two of them. There would be less fear in his life if he began again somewhere else. Perhaps there was something to the Chinese superstition of not buying or living in a house in which a person had died. She allowed him the luxury of sacrifice. He honored the unspoken rules of conduct between former lovers. Aurora knew he suffered and he understood. Acceptance, but no pity. His leaving was love, his sacrifice was love, his pride was love, his return was love, his silence was love.

Weeks later, Aurora was sitting on the edge of the bed, combing her wet hair, when the phone rang. She didn't move to answer it, and the machine picked up instead. When she heard Raymond's voice, she pulled the bathrobe close around her. He sounded distracted. He admitted there was no reason he had called, then said there was a reason, but he had forgotten what it was. Then he remembered that he had called to tell her his new phone number, but he didn't leave the number. He would call again.

5 sleepwalking

AT FIRST THEIR PARTING, THEIR SEPARATION, THEIR
movement away from each other, was not absolute and final. They
accepted each other on ever-changing terms, broke down barriers,
reset borders, traveled together, shared unspoken regrets, made
agreements, and made love for the last time several times.

There was time and distance between them. Each time they got
together, each of them measured and gauged the silence between
them. Each time was a kind of starting over. Both of them experienced a weightlessness when their relationship ended, making
them friends instead of lovers. There was a formality in the asking
of a favor, making an appointment, seeking advice; and with acceptance or resignation, their answer, their gratefulness, was without pride, without hope of a return to the way lovers speak. Was
it possible to understand what specific kindness was friendship
rather than condescension, or genuine sentimentality rather than
emotional fatigue? They both wondered if they were going forward. If they were, was there a brink out there on the horizon? Was
the field flat now? Which one was pushing, or leading, or waiting?
Was it impossible to fall?

It was what Aurora became after Raymond left that split their
image, divided her from him, separated cultures, as if they had

mixed blood with paint. She called it *identity* in her photographs. They documented her time without him and took possession of anything that he had left behind. They captured sound, recalled conversations, and understood or explained her half-Japanese, half-white familial roots. In one of her photographs a porcelain headrest fell to the ground during a fitful sleep and shattered. She had titled it "His Absence." His absence pulled her, at first, into the vacuum, the space where he had been. His absence later defined her, gave her black-and-white images, sound and touch as well as shape. Her photographs told a story of a teardrop falling into a pan of hot oil, a jade bracelet knocking against a hot iron, a bucket clanging against the side of a well. After each departure, less and less of his presence remained in her home, until all the space he had once occupied became hers. Every woman she saw became a symbol for the place she occupied, the home she defined around herself, the roots that she set down. She saw herself span several generations. She was a woman who wrung out a shirt between two strong hands, a woman who plunged a cleaver into the breast of a chicken, a woman who pulled open an iron door and took a heated stone from beneath a fire-heated brick bed and slept with the warm stone on her belly on a winter night. She was a woman who scolded a child and watched a tear fall into a pan of hot oil and pop in the heat.

A camera shutter opened and closed in 1/500th of a second. In another photograph, a woman spoke. "I am my father's first son," she said.

Along the border of one photograph, Aurora had written in pencil: "A son marries, raises children, and his first son carries the family into the next generation. A cook says, 'Feed wood or the shells of turtles to the son; he will inherit longevity.' 'If I eat the turtle,' the son replies, 'he dies.' The cook shrugs. 'He passes his life on to you.' A son's life is dominated by such symbols."

◆ ◆ ◆

ONE DAY, FOR NO REASON, Aurora called her own phone number, listened to the message on her answering machine, and after the beep, asked, "Raymond, are you there? If you are, please pick up the phone." She was embarrassed by the neediness in her voice. Then she felt ridiculous, calling her own empty apartment, but she waited on the line. The background noise from the newsroom occupied the answering machine's sensors and kept it from disconnecting her. She knew she would feel silly listening to the message later. At least, she thought, only she would know how weak she was. She turned a page of the magazine in front of her with the eraser tip of her pencil. She wanted to say something to remind herself of what she had lost or what she had gained. A second line at her desk rang, but she didn't answer it.

He shouldn't have been there, but he was. He listened to her voice. He tried to think of a reason why he was in their, no, her apartment without her knowledge. He told himself that she knew he still had a key. She wanted him to keep one "in case of an emergency." She knew he had too much pride to use the key unannounced, to intrude in a life that he no longer shared. When he picked up the phone, he had no excuse.

She didn't wait for him to stumble over one, instead invited him to dinner and asked him to make some rice. "It's in the same place," she told him, and said she would stop in Chinatown on her way home to buy a fish and some vegetables.

After they hung up, they were both dismayed at the exhibition of their own weakness for each other. Immediately each of them planned for the talk they would have later and planned how not to talk about their mutual lapse.

When Aurora came home she was comforted by the smell of steamed rice in the apartment. Raymond could have his talk of eth-

nicity and ethnic politics. The most reaffirming act Aurora knew
was making rice, the task that began every meal.

He wasn't home. Aurora looked for a note in the place where he
usually left notes. Had he had second thoughts? Was his pride hurt
at having been caught in the apartment? Aurora set her bags down
in the kitchen, walked to the bay windows in the kitchen, and
opened them. The curtains billowed in. She pushed them aside and
looked out. Raymond was walking up the street, a newspaper in
one hand and a pink box from the bakery in the other. Aurora
waved but didn't say anything. She opened the front door so that
Raymond wouldn't have to decide whether to knock or use his key.
She boiled water for tea and began to clean the fish.

"I went out to buy a newspaper," Raymond said before walking
into the kitchen. "There's an interesting story about the drought."

"Raymond," Aurora said above the sound of the water running
into the sink, "I work for a newspaper. You know I bring home two
copies every day." The apartment seemed to have become smaller
since Raymond moved out, and the two of them were standing
face-to-face before Aurora had finished her sentence. She repeated
in a lower voice, as if she were recuing her timing, "Two copies
every day—"

"I bought dessert."

"—morning edition and night final."

She looked at the box, then at Raymond. She knew what was in
the box. Peach pie or glazed fruit tarts. *All the things we know about
each other, we can't unlearn.* What should he have done—gone out and
purposefully misjudged what she liked to eat for dessert? Perhaps
buying the newspaper was a gesture toward unlearning, toward becoming something else in her life.

"It's a peach pie."

Aurora looked at Raymond. He felt suddenly foolish, pathetic
and at the same time too aggressive. Her look told him that she

wanted to be able to live without him. She turned away from him, leaving the fish in the sink with the water running, and sat at the kitchen table. "I just wanted you to make rice."

It wasn't fair to expect him not to know things about her, not to remember a passion for peach pie or her taste in clothes, not to be able to read her mind, not to know that there was a reason they often said the same things at the same time. Even his holding back from demonstrating his complete knowledge of her was as much a threat and an invasion as a reassurance and a comfort.

Raymond sat down across the table from Aurora. "Do you ever find it difficult to explain to other people what happened to us?" Without waiting for an answer, he continued, "Don't you wish there were some easy little ten-second sound bite we could use? Something so ordinary and mundane that as soon as we mentioned it, people would understand. 'Ah, yes, I see,' they would say. 'He was sleeping with your best friend. She fell in love with her personal trainer. He was abusive. She wanted to get married and you weren't ready to settle down. He was threatened by your independence. She's having another guy's baby. He was married and he didn't tell you. She fell in love with a woman. He was immature and spoiled. He was lousy in bed. She was a bitch. You stopped communicating. You wanted to see other people. You outgrew each other.'"

Aurora didn't interrupt. When he finished his list, they fell silent. They listened to the water running in the sink. They cradled empty teacups in their hands like fragile eggs.

"You know the reason, Raymond."

"So you say."

"I can't be exactly what you want me to be."

"But that's the point." Raymond pushed his teacup to the middle of the table. "I was only offering you the ability to be what you are."

Aurora wanted to say, *Who I am, not what I am*, but they had been through all this before. Raymond had become, on a more complicated level, like the people who asked Aurora what she was and where she came from. The ignorant were rude; Raymond was educational.

When the water boiled for the tea, Raymond rose and turned off the stove, got the tea from the cupboard, pinched some leaves between his fingers and dropped them into the pot, and poured the water. He watched the dry tea leaves float to the surface. Before they sank to the bottom, Raymond placed his set of keys to Aurora's apartment on the stove next to the tea and left.

Down on the sidewalk, in front of Aurora's apartment, an Asian woman passed him. She was wearing a T-shirt that read, "It's an Asian thing. You wouldn't understand." She caught him reading the slogan across her chest and smiled as if he understood.

A pain settled on him, a simple despair invaded the air around him. His car was parked at the top of the hill in the block above the apartment. Instead of climbing the hill to his car, Raymond let the pain push him down the hill and away. Once, Aurora had rescued him from pain.

Let the tea steep.

Let the water run in the sink.

There's a story about the drought.

UP IN HER KITCHEN, Aurora whispered for no reason, "It leaves something to be desired." She crossed to the sink and watched the water run down the drain.

She would miss the kissing.

Their first kiss had been awkward, slightly hard-lipped, perhaps too loaded with anticipation and fantasy, each of them trying to impress upon the other the meaning of their connection. Aurora's lips were slightly more pliable than his, as if she had shouldered the responsibility for the eleven-year difference in their ages. She thought about how some men kissed like they had learned to kiss by watching James Bond movies and fishing shows on television, coming at her with their mouths open. Some men were imitative and allowed themselves to be led by example. Raymond preferred to take turns kissing.

Later, on his return to D.C., Aurora had met him at the airport. In the lounge by the arrival gate, Raymond said, "Kiss me." He said it with finality, because he feared that in person the relationship wouldn't survive all the inevitable explanations of his failed marriage, disclaimers about his age, and warnings about the distance between them. He wanted to remember the kiss of her as a lover before she decided to kiss him as a friend. Aurora sat on his lap and kissed his cheek. The touch of her lips on his cheek was light and wet, and as her lips pulled away he heard her faint breath through her open mouth. She touched the spot where she had kissed him and kissed his mouth even more lightly, as if only the moisture between their lips should touch, as if their lips were liquid. Before Raymond could speak, Aurora pulled him to his feet, saying, "Let's catch a cab home."

In Aurora's apartment, Raymond's lips had lost the words of his narrative about his life, his age, her youth, her innocence (something he had overestimated). When he started to kiss her, he began with the palm of her hand and the inside of her forearm for no reason at all. Then her shoulder, through the silk of her blouse. *I'll pay for the dry cleaning later*, he thought. He placed his warm palm inside the open neckline and unbuttoned it, then traced the outline of her clavicle with his tongue and lips. Aurora did not remember Raymond unbuttoning her blouse and unhooking her bra. He seemed not to touch her with anything except his lips. She felt weightless. His hands applied no pressure on her bare skin. She found herself remembering the teenage boys who had pressed their hands up her skirt or kneaded her breasts or grabbed her hands and forced them into their unzipped flies.

"Say something," Aurora had said. "Put me somewhere." As if he were a drug.

Raymond licked the underside of her breast. He saw goose bumps rise on Aurora's bare chest and stomach. He watched her breathe and thought about what she was asking him. "Where?" he asked. He touched a nipple with the tip of his tongue and kissed it, then the other one.

"Take me somewhere."

Raymond was not sure what she meant. Did she want to move to another room? Could he carry her?

"Somewhere?" he whispered.

With her eyes closed she nodded, but Raymond didn't know if it was in response to the question or in response to his kissing the rising and falling of her stomach as she breathed. He looked around the room. It was humid; and all the windows were open. The white curtains were billowing in and out.

"Tell me a story."

Raymond wasn't sure he could be creative and stay hard.

"It's very humid today."

Aurora nodded again.

Finally he understood what she wanted.

Someone has told us that it's going to rain even though it's hot and sunny. There is a breeze today like the trade winds in Hawaii. I've got the windows open in two rooms, the study and the bedroom. The white curtains are billowing in and out.

RAYMOND SURVEYED THE ROOM and imagined something else. It wasn't Aurora's fantasy but his own.

It's the kind of lazy, hot afternoon where we walk through the rooms naked. You're on the bed, reading. You've pushed all the blankets off the bed because you like the coolness of the crisp white sheets against your skin. It's better not to move too much on a day like today. You read, you doze, you read. I'm sitting at the desk, writing a letter. Then I hear you in the bedroom next to the study. Are you talking to yourself, dreaming, or talking on the telephone? When I check on you, you are sleeping and saying something in your dreams. I sit in a chair and watch you sleep. Suddenly I think what you are dreaming is erotic, because I am hard. I should make love to you now, but I'd rather watch you. I want you to wake and see me hard and come to me and take me in your mouth. You turn over on your stomach and I can see your hand between your legs. What are you saying? Is it me you're dreaming about? Your fingers are wet. I want to push your legs apart and enter you. Say something. You want to feel me come. Say something. I want to watch you dream. Say something. I hear you whisper you are not asleep.

AURORA HAD FELT THE PRESSURE of Raymond's hands, and with her own she had guided him.

There was a touch Raymond had that told Aurora that he wanted her. Raymond didn't know when he used it. It was the way he sometimes placed his hand around her ribs just below her breast as they crossed the street, or held a part of her body that he usually didn't grab, like her wrist and not her hand, or the inside of her upper arm. It was a possessive touch, as if she needed to be guided. It was always in public.

If she quizzed him about his possession of her, Raymond would speak of the times he touched her breast or placed his hand in the crotch of her jeans or let his hand slip down to her ass or rested his hand under the weight of her thigh while she was driving. Manly fantasies of public possession. Aurora saw it in the way he sometimes looked at other women. Most times she simply noticed a curiosity or an admiration in his look, but it was a detached look. She read his mind: *nice tits, great legs, short skirt*. Possession had to do with confidence. Sometimes Raymond looked at women with the same confidence with which he guided her across a street, a crowded room, a slippery floor. She wanted to make love with him then, not when he was being obvious.

THERE WAS AN ENDING TO THIS, but Aurora didn't want it to end like this. She looked at the empty teacups on the table and the teapot on the stove. At the sink, she watched the water run over the fish. She turned on the garbage disposal, listened to it spinning freely, then pushed the fish down it.

Men were always more predictable to Aurora when she left them. At some point they would always say how much she meant to them. Raymond was slow in proving his predictability. He returned too many times. He wanted to show rather than tell Aurora how much she meant to him. Talk about relationships always sounded like a cliché. He tried to be original. Aurora wanted the freedom of the clichés.

Aurora thought about where her relationship with Raymond took its place among the others. When it came time for her to talk about him in the past tense, with other women or even other men, would he be part of a group simply titled "my old boyfriends"? Where would she reserve her feelings about him? Would she only dwell on the details about how they misconnected, miscommunicated, misunderstood? It was ironic to her that the agreement to separate was where lovers finally found their common ground and compliance, their compromise and resignation.

MONTHS LATER, in their separate beds, Raymond and Aurora dreamed about making love. The details of their lovemaking woke them from their sleep. Were they with someone else? Were they alone? In her bed, Aurora turned and recognized the man she was with. Raymond was alone. In their separate beds and separate homes, each of them realized that it wasn't a dream that had disturbed their sleep, but rather a memory.

This was what she remembered. After making love, Aurora held Raymond inside her, pressed him deep inside her, and controlled her breathing and her movement so as not to lose him as his erection faded. She kept him inside of her until at last he slid out and their breathing took on separate rhythms. The humidity between their bodies evaporated.

At the precise moment Raymond separated himself from her, Aurora's body replayed how her orgasm began. Sometimes she wanted the feeling to begin again immediately. She straddled his leg and placed her hand on his cock and held him firmly. Raymond pushed her hand down around the base of his cock and his balls until the sensitivity dissipated. Aurora liked holding Raymond like this. He was as wet as she was. Aurora's wetness coated the insides of his thighs as it did her own thighs. She wanted to make love again. She wanted the way Raymond concentrated completely on her orgasm the second time. She stroked his thigh with her wet hand. She waited.

But how did it begin? What was the recollection that woke them? It began when she was combing her wet hair in the bathroom after stepping from the shower. Raymond unwrapped the towel from around her and dried her back. She watched his blurred image in the steamed mirror. He knelt down and dried her legs; the back of his hand pushed up against her pussy. If she laughed, they moved on to their morning coffee. Aurora didn't laugh, didn't complain. Raymond dropped the towel and, still on his knees, turned her around, and as he stood he lifted her up on the bathroom counter and pushed her legs apart. He nuzzled her wet pubic hair. Aurora smelled like soap. He pressed his tongue inside her. She asked Raymond if he wanted to be inside her, and felt him shake his head. She reached for support on the counter and knocked a bottle into the sink. Later, the crystal stopper in the bottle slid out and they were consumed by a vapor.

Aurora remembered that they had laughed afterward about how she hit the faucet when she came. Raymond said he heard waves. Lying in bed in the dark, Raymond remembered the perfumed air that cascaded down. Aurora's body when she came. Neither of them could sleep. Aurora was wet, but she was with someone else. Raymond began to masturbate as if the dream he had could be frozen into a two-dimensional photo of their lust, but his erection faded as soon as his memory replaced the dream. He made coffee instead.

Drinking it, he stared at his unmade bed and remembered how every morning after Aurora rose, he would roll over and occupy the spot she left. She had the perfumed scent, the better dreams, the greater heat.

His body fit into the impression she left behind.

6 fear of flying

BRENDA NISHITANI REFUSED TO UNDERSTAND WHY SHE
and Aurora were attending the annual fund-raising dinner and art
auction for the Office of Minority Affairs at Jack London College.
She had said, while she was waiting to check her coat, that when
relationships are over they are over.

"It's our civic duty to support the college," Aurora said.

"Oh, good." Brenda gave Aurora a look. "I thought we were
here because you're still in love with the Chinaman."

"Buy some art, Brenda."

She and Brenda had arrived during the preview and cocktail
hour. When Raymond saw them he greeted them, kissed Aurora on
the cheek, shook Brenda's hand, then changed his mind and gave
her a hug. He had their name tags in his pocket and pointed to their
table. After he left to continue greeting people, Brenda had said,
"Isn't he just a little too cheerful and helpful?" With his back
turned, Raymond heard Brenda's comment, and to himself he had
added, *and obsequious.*

Brenda watched Raymond work the room as if she were waiting for some evidence in his behavior that would finally liberate
Aurora from his influence. When she caught Raymond getting a
kiss and a hug from a white woman with bad hair and Birken-

stocks, she nudged Aurora and pointed with her glass. "It's disgusting to see an Asian man with an ugly white woman," she said, looking away from Raymond so that Aurora wouldn't be too hurt.

Aurora watched the display of affection. "That isn't his girlfriend. She works with him. Her name's Astral Anitra. She's married, with two children."

"Sounds like a fake name."

"It is. Her name used to be Shirley Greenberg. Anitra means duck in Italian."

"Pegged her," Brenda said, then turned to look in Raymond's direction again. "I'm not a racist, Ro. I'm not saying all white women are ugly when they're with Asian men. You know what I mean. It's the Asian guy so desperate to smack up skin-to-skin with a white girl he picks anyone who'll have him. Or the nice-looking ones who look kind of guilty when you stare at them."

"Maybe it's because of the way your mouth gets all twisted up in that sneer," Aurora added.

"They look like they've been caught in the headlights and don't know which way to run."

"That's fright, not guilt."

"For Asian boys there's no difference."

Brenda pointed at another couple, a handsome Asian man with a truly gorgeous white girl. "Then there are the ones with some awesome Barbie babe with the blond curly mane and the legs and the tits, great beach material. Those boys just stare you down or ignore you, like, 'Go ahead and hit me with your headlights; I'm indestructible.' He's with the woman all men lust after. Hell, she's the kind of girl we wanted to be when we were thumbing through the pages of *Seventeen*, while mom's telling us the advantages of straight black hair."

"He's very cute, Brenda."

"Sure he's cute, but I just don't understand the attraction."

"What about the ugly nerd Asian boy and the beautiful white girl?" Aurora asked, scanning the room for an example.

"I don't mind. I'm not threatened. No love or lust there. It's a charity case, or more likely it's study hall time. She needs a passing grade in calculus in order to stay on the cheerleading squad. Henry's there to help. He has his day in the sun. Then he melts, unless he's too rich to melt."

"Why do you care, Brenda?" Aurora asked, eyeing Astral, who was still clinging to Raymond. "You don't go out with Asian men."

It was a question that didn't need an answer. Aurora had heard Brenda's theories on Asian men and Asian women before. Brenda always said she tried to date Asian men but didn't know how. She was *sansei* and grew up in the suburbs, where there were no Asian boys. She didn't want to be Japanese; she wanted to be like all the other kids. In college she was in a sorority, and there weren't any Asian guys in the frats. She got invited to some Chinese Student Association dances but felt out of place. A lot of the Chinese girls froze her out because she was a Japanese sorority girl from the suburbs. She couldn't relate when "Orientals" suddenly became "Asian Americans" and began taking ethnic studies classes, going into Chinatown clothing stores and buying *mee nahps*, taking judo and karate lessons, eating *poi*, and spelling out nonnegotiable demands on a bullhorn in front of the administration building.

Once she had gone on a date with a Korean guy, but both sets of parents nearly went on full tilt just thinking about the Japanese-Korean thing. The mutual stereotypes were too much to overcome: Japan's invasion and occupation of Korea—they had enslaved Korean women during World War II—versus Koreans' monolithic rudeness and abrupt manner.

Japanese practiced *gaman* and *enryo*, meaning nobody took the last piece of chicken no matter what; let it go uneaten back to the kitchen, defer and be patient. Fight over the bill until you tear it in

half. Send a thank you card as soon as you get home. Next time excuse yourself to go to the bathroom and pay the bill secretly in the
back. Chinese scrimped on things at home, clipped coupons,
never bought retail—warehouse stores were made for them—but
they, too, would fight to the death over the bill. Gave them "big
face."

In Washington, Brenda went out with a couple of black guys,
but she couldn't handle the vicious looks and backbiting from the
black women she met, some of it loud enough for her and her date
to hear. "Got hisself a yearning for high yellowness so high he got
a Chink." The chorus behind her voiced their *uh huhs*. If you
couldn't fight back, you couldn't survive in that environment. One
time Brenda and one of the women got into it so deep that
Brenda's date had to step between them. Over his shoulder Brenda
said something about the woman's mother. Brenda's date got a
black eye.

The Korean and black experiences made her dad easier to handle
when she moved back to California and started dating white boys
again.

"Asian men *do* have great bodies," Brenda said, "but I don't
want to date them, or have sex with them, or marry them. We've
been married to them for four thousand years. Let someone else
do it."

Brenda just liked the way they looked—the hairlessness, the
Bruce Lee muscle tone. Brenda liked going to kung fu movies and
samurai movies, liked her Asian men virile and heroic and strong.
To that extent she was loyal to the race. And as much as she put
Asian men down as mates to Aurora, she would defend them
against racist remarks in public.

"Too bad white guys can't have Asian bodies," Brenda said,
pointing at a white guy across the room. "I hate chest hair and hairy
backs. God, I hope I don't end up married to some white guy who

wears his jeans so low that the crack of his hairy white ass shows when he bends down."

"Too bad Bruce Lee had that accent," Aurora added.

"Yeah, too bad." Wistfulness.

Brenda was secretly delighted by Aurora's comment. It had been a long time since they could talk so freely. It was almost impossible to be politically incorrect, even in jest, living with Raymond. Aurora had learned in nauseating detail how to talk about "people of color," including herself among them.

It wasn't that Brenda was insensitive to Asian American issues. She was simply capable of separating questions of loyalty to the race from her personal everyday life. In her everyday life, Brenda liked the Thai boys at the Thai Takeout because they were polite and had beautifully smooth skin. The mother of the family that ran the takeout looked young enough to be the boys' sister. Brenda often wondered if they could dance.

Streetwise Vietnamese and other recent immigrant boys were always staring at Asian American women like Brenda who shopped in their grocery stores, coming up to them and saying, "Hi, how are you?" with an accent that began with forming their mouths as if each word started with an O. Sometimes they walked up to Brenda dragging the heels of their shoes on the floor, which drove her crazy. She wanted to yell, "Pick up your feet!" They wanted to know what she was, to see if it was OK to go out with her. "Are you Chinese? I'm Vietnamese Chinese." Sometimes she tried to be friendly and joke with them, but they laughed two beats too late. They strained too hard to make casual conversation out of what Brenda bought, what she ate, what she drank, and what magazines she read. When she bought aspirin, they wanted to know if she was "making a headache." She never bought tampons from them.

Brenda's aunt had married a white man during the war, when she was released from Minidoka Relocation Center to go back to school in Chicago. She said it was better for the kids, so that the next time the country wanted to round up the Japanese and haul them off to camp, they wouldn't be able to recognize them, like the Germans and the Italians who got off easy during the war. Brenda's aunt said the sooner the Japanese married out, the better. The whole country was going to be Hispanic in a few years; maybe all Asians could pass for Hispanic in a generation or two, then pass for white after that, even change their names, like the Jews and the Mexicans.

Brenda's aunt said the kids got it all wrong in the sixties with their endless search for identity and their self-determination crap. "What is it you kids don't know? Why do you want to draw attention to yourself? You kids didn't even know we were in camp until you read about it in your high school textbooks. Then you come home wearing black armbands, wanting to know why we never told you about the camps. You never asked."

Brenda's aunt and uncle took their kids to Disney World with the twenty-thousand-dollar redress money and bought a new fishing boat they named *Camp Harmony*, after the first camp she had been sent to. (The War Relocation Authority had called it an "assembly center," but in reality it was the livestock stall at the county fairgrounds.) Meanwhile editorial pages of every newspaper in America were filled with letters from readers who protested the payments and wanted to know if redress would be paid to the "Americans" who died at Pearl Harbor.

"You know, Brenda, the men aren't the problem. Seventy-five percent of Japanese American women are marrying out of the race, compared to twenty percent of the men," Aurora said, pointing to herself as a product of this statistic. "So the odds favor your becoming one of those hyphenated women—a Nishitani-Miller, or a Nishitani-Polanski, or a Nishitani-Washington."

"Nishitani-Washington—now there's a thought, Ro."

Aurora wondered if black men who have a thing for Asian women were less likely to be racist than white men who have a thing for Asian women.

Brenda scanned the room. "I like black coffee, black silk, little black dresses, black tights, black shoes, black leather pants, oversize black T-shirts, black bras, black cars, black squid linguine."

Aurora nudged Brenda and pointed to a man who was circulating through the room, handing out auction catalogs and assigning bidding numbers.

"Oh, shit," Brenda said. "Let's find our table and sit down."

Glenn Tompkins was the opposite of hip black squid linguine and black bras. Brenda had gone out with him once. At first everybody in the Asian community called him "Red." It was a real cliché because of his red hair, and no one who had grown up in Chinatown or Japantown had ever gotten to call anyone "Red." Fresh out of Stanford, with an Asian Studies degree, Glenn floated between Chinatown and Japantown, dabbling in things Chinese and Japanese and trying to hang with the guys. For a while rumor had it that Glenn was gay, a rice queen. Asian men wouldn't even walk on the same side of the street. When they found out he was after the women, they didn't mind his presence.

Glenn joined the Japanese Buddhist Church, volunteered to drive the church van and take the old-timers out for their excursions, cooked for the bazaar potluck, buddied up to the *nisei* aunts who might introduce him to their daughters, tutored English down at the Chinatown community service center, and took Chinese and Japanese language classes until he knew more Chinese and Japanese than most of the girls he tried to date. Glenn was not some Midwest sailor who, on R & R in Hong Kong the first time away from the family farm, got a taste of some Oriental poontang and a massage and put himself on the waiting list for "Oriental girls" back home. He knew the difference between a stereotypical Hollywood image of an Asian woman and a real Asian American woman. He was more comfortable being a white guy immersed in a culture he could study and understand, instead of being what he was—part Scottish, Irish, French, and, the inevitable, one-sixteenth Cherokee. A lot of Asian women had gone out with him once, but he didn't know that he fell into the same category as the other boys their aunts set them up with—a boring wimp and, in this case, a boring wimp who wanted to talk about Asian culture.

"Who's that sitting at our table?" Brenda asked as they approached.

Aurora checked the table number on her name tag and the number on the table again, then sighed. "It's Raymond's friend Jimmy Chan. He's the editor of the *National Asian American Weekly*. He's always making a big deal about me being a photographer for the establishment *San Francisco Examiner*. My talents, he says, should be put toward *the cause*."

Brenda groaned. "Is he an FOB?"

Aurora shook her head. "Born right here in Oakland."

"He looks like an immigrant." Brenda watched him closely, then pointed. "Look: he's even got that immigrant involuntary nervous bouncing knee thing."

"That's not an immigrant thing, Brenda."

"Well, it's an Asian male thing. It's the only way their bodies know how to release their repressed feelings."

Aurora had to agree but felt obligated to defend him. "He actually writes some good editorials. His most recent one was an attack on racist depictions of Asian men on television and in the movies. He pointed out how Chinese men rarely get to play real men."

"They rule by proverb, not brawn."

"Yes. Of course, most of the time, Chinese men have been played by white actors in yellowface, with latex-slanted eyes."

"Listen, Ro, David Carradine is wimpy even when he's playing a white guy."

Aurora continued. "Jimmy wrote that on *Bonanza* a white woman would be shy about showing her ankle to Hoss or Little Joe, but she could walk around Hop Sing's kitchen with her corset on without fear. Everyone knew nothing would happen to her. He's no real man. Jimmy said movie apes have made bigger strides in self-determination than Chinese, going from King Kong pounding on the gates of Skull Island to speaking and taking over the world in *Planet of the Apes*, while Chinese have gone from Charlie Chan to Hop Sing." Brenda pointed at Jimmy. "I wouldn't walk around in my corset in front of him."

"You walk around in a corset in front of any man and it will drive them crazy," Aurora said.

Brenda was tall, long-legged, short-waisted, and had large breasts. Her breasts she got from her mother, but otherwise her mother and father were short, bow-legged, and long-waisted. Brenda's mother said vitamins and stretching her limbs were what did it. At Brenda's birth she had been relieved to see that her daughter had all her toes and fingers, and double eyelids as well. For good measure, she had pinched infant Brenda's nose to make it thin. Brenda was going to be an all-American girl.

"They shouldn't give Asian women large breasts, because we have enough problems as it is," Brenda had once said to Aurora. "In American culture, the boobs become your identity. Even Asian women mention it. Men come up to me and actually point at my breasts and say, 'Oriental girls don't usually have those.'"

"Don't worry about Jimmy; he's married," Aurora added.

"Who'd marry him?" Brenda shook her head. "I mean, look at him. Is there some book somewhere that tells Asian men how to accentuate their long-waisted bodies and short legs by wearing vertically striped shirts? No wonder they have names like Hop Sing in

the movies instead of Bo or Leroy or Scarface. And leave it to someone like him to try and guilt a beautiful woman into working at his
rag instead of coming right out and asking you to work for him.
And they wonder why we marry white guys."

Aurora waited for Brenda to finish pounding the subject into the
ground.

"Actually, Ro, the best of both worlds would be to marry a
white guy and have one-hundred-percent-Asian babies because
they're so cute. Even white women who marry Asian men want
one-hundred-percent Asian babies."

"Brenda," Aurora interrupted, "you're a mass of contradictions."

"Hey, you know as well as I do that even white couples with
their own little white children want to adopt Korean babies."

"Go buy some art, Brenda."

Brenda took the hint and made her way toward the room where
the art was being previewed.

"Hello, Jimmy," Aurora said, taking a seat five chairs away from
him at the round table.

"I didn't expect to see you here," he said, scanning the room.
"What with you and Raymond and all."

Aurora wanted to explain she had been invited by Raymond.
Instead she said only, "I'm supporting the cause." The statement
came spilling out of a liquid nitrogen bottle, and if she had taken a
little hammer out of her purse and given Jimmy a tap at that moment, he should have shattered all over the floor. But somehow he
wouldn't freeze.

"What's your friend's name again?" As if he didn't know.

Aurora wondered why men always pretended to not know the
name of a beautiful woman. The slight twitch in Jimmy's eyebrows
said it all.

"Brenda." *Not in your wildest dreams*, she thought. She stood up
and walked toward the preview room.

RAYMOND JOINED JIMMY AT THE TABLE.

"Look at that guy," Jimmy said, pointing across the room with his chin. Raymond turned and saw a young Asian man who might have been Vietnamese walking hand in hand with a young white woman with bleached-blond hair. "He must have watched too many reruns of *Gilligan's Island*. It was a long search, but he found Ginger. Mom and Dad must be pleased with him. The American Dream. Shit, man, FOB's be stealin' our women."

This biting sarcasm rarely appeared in Jimmy's editorials, but Raymond knew him to be particularly treacherous when it came to intra-Asian commentary.

"What did Aurora say to you?" Raymond asked.

Jimmy shrugged. "She was being frosty. She reminds me of my bank teller. Why is it every time I go to the bank to withdraw cash and I get an Asian woman teller, she's got to go in the back and check my signature and my bank balance? I've been banking at the same bank for years, and they got two Asian women tellers. They know me. I give them a break and think maybe I've got an attitude. So I go up to the window of this one woman all friendly like and look at her nameplate and call her by her name: 'Hey, Suzanna, how are you doing today?' She says, 'Fine,' like a robot, and before I can speak again she spins around and heads for the back."

"You're being paranoid," Raymond said, even though he knew what Jimmy meant. "Maybe she's got a crush on you. Likes to have you linger around. Wants to see if you got enough money to keep her happy."

"I know what it is: they're prejudiced."

"Why is it," Raymond joined in, "every time I get on an airplane and walk down the jetway to the plane, I see ten, twelve people walk by the flight attendant and she stops me and wants to see my boarding pass? Is it because I'm cute and she wants to make small talk? Is it because she thinks I'm sitting in first class and she wants to greet me? No! She thinks I can't read or speak English and I might be getting on the wrong damn plane, that I'm too stupid to match flight numbers! These days I make it a point of walking right up to them and saying, 'Howdy! Howzit goin' today? Hope we'll have a humdinger of a flight?'"

Others had joined them at the table, and Jimmy continued with a riff Raymond had heard before. "The worst is when I'm given a seat next to another Asian. The flight attendant automatically thinks the two 'Orientals' are together. If he or she is from China somewhere I don't really care. Maybe I can even help them out with the English. And they're relieved."

Raymond pointed at Jimmy and started to laugh. "Except when they realize you can't speak Chinese all that well. It's why foreign-born Chinese call American-born Chinese *jook sing*, hollow bamboo; me and you look Chinese, but we're hollow inside, no substance."

Jimmy knocked his head and made a hollow sound by clicking his tongue. "We're in deep shit when the other passenger's an Asian American woman. The flight attendant is going to come by and ask, 'What would you two like to drink?' Everybody gets irritated by the assumption. It becomes a contest of body language that says, *I'm not with him, I don't know him, I speak English, I don't date Asian men because they're domineering wimps.* 'No, I don't want tea. I'll have coffee—black.'"

Raymond played the straight man to Jimmy's tirade. "Then there's the Asian woman with the white husband who have been assigned the seats next to you."

"They go through this dance thing where they're trying to figure out who is going to sit next to whom. What makes the best sense. We're all standing in the aisle trying to be polite, trying to suppress the fear in our eyes and the apologies for even considering the questions. I want to tell the woman that I've got no problem with her marrying a white guy. I'm a nice guy. I want to make small talk with her husband about sports and regular-guy stuff. But I can't say anything. Finally the woman sits by the window, I sit on the aisle and there's this oversize hairy white guy sitting between us, like a human demilitarized zone. I'm looking to see if there's an empty seat nearby next to a pair with a more manageable color combination."

"Exactly." Raymond sighed. "Except we move to another seat to keep everyone from feeling ashamed, guilty, or defensive." He had sat in all three of those seats.

BRENDA AND AURORA SURVEYED THE ART and made notations in their catalogs about the items they might bid on.

"The men," Brenda told Aurora, "aren't our problem. We've essentially left them behind. You say we're marrying out seventy-five percent. What about them? Who keeps track of them? Who cares?"

"Well, I think we should care, whether or not we want to marry them. I think it has some impact on us as Asian Americans."

"You were with Raymond too long. This sounds like one of his lectures."

"Maybe it's not them we're so against. Maybe it's the thought of having two sets of Asian parents like our own. Maybe we're afraid the boys we marry will grow up to be our domineering fathers."

"Maybe it's like kissing your brother," countered Brenda.

"Name an Asian American celebrity couple," Aurora demanded.

Brenda pondered. "Mr. and Mrs. I. M. Pei."

"You're guessing."

"You name one."

"Name a celebrity mixed marriage where the husband is Asian."

Brenda bit her bottom lip, deep in thought. "Is Yo-Yo Ma married to a white woman?"

"If I were to ask you to name a celebrity mixed marriage where the woman is Asian, you'd have a whole list, led by—"

"Connie Chung and Maury Povich!"

"Our acceptance is as much a product of stereotype as the Asian man's ostracism as an unmanly wimp. The media exploit our sexuality. Name a middle-aged Asian American actress. You can't."

"It's not my fault; it's our culture. There aren't any older white-haired white women news reporters either. You have to be blond and young, while the men can be shriveled up and nearing retirement; in them it's called integrity, media confidence, and experience."

"Speaking of Connie," Aurora added, "there aren't any Asian male anchors on television news. Why?"

"They're not believable spokesmen? They're shifty and sneaky? You can't see their eyes when they smile?"

"Be serious."

"Okay, Aurora. Are we supposed to change the world for our men? What do you want me to do about a culture that says Asian women are beautiful and acceptable and Asian men aren't? Remember that nude photo of Burt Reynolds in *Cosmo* that launched his career? In all the editions outside of America, they featured a Eurasian man. Is it so bad that America has a little hang-up about Asian men's masculinity, while the rest of the world seems to be pretty straight about it? You want him to be the Marlboro man or something?"

"Out in the real world," Aurora proposed, "what do you take offense with first—race or gender issues?"

"Did you think of any of these things before meeting Raymond?"

"Of course I did! And each time, for me, it was race prejudice first and often, while the level of sexism was a constant part of our culture. Maybe because I'm *hapa*, as the Hawaiians say—you know, half—people are more curious and obnoxious about how they ask, 'What are you?'"

"Is this a panel discussion, Aurora? Are white male fantasies about Asian femininity racist or sexist? I don't think we can draw a straight line."

"If you play up to a man's ideal fantasy of Asian femininity, then you're a racist, and he's a racist and a sexist!"

"How can I be a racist? I'm an Asian American woman!"

"Uh huh."

"I don't really have anything against Asian men. You know I've gone on dates with them. But it always seems at some point on the date, both of us are thinking that this is what we're supposed to be doing, that it is right and proper. It's actually a relief that neither one of us wants to go to a Chinese or Japanese restaurant for dinner, and we can laugh about that. It's not much of a struggle. It's a match."

"Uh huh."

"Maybe relationships need more differences in order to make them work in today's world. In our parents' world they were planning families, working the farm together, or living in enclaves like Japantown and Chinatown. They didn't venture out into the world because the world kept them on the fringe. The doors are open now, we have access. No one is stopping the men from having access. There aren't any antimiscegenation laws anymore. They can marry out. I just don't know why they have to marry out ugly. Maybe it's got more to do with self-contempt than racism. We bring it on ourselves because we feel we're not worth more."

"Look who's doing the ethnic studies lecture now."

"I'm on a roll, Aurora." Brenda took a deep breath. "Raymond's a sexy guy. You know that; I know that. I think he's cute."

"For a Chinese guy, you mean," Aurora added.

"Look at him." Brenda looked for Raymond but couldn't spot him. "He doesn't look like a typical bad-driving Chinese guy. He's got good cheekbones, big eyes that don't disappear when he smiles, thin nose. He's tall. Good haircut. His legs are a little short. Good clothes. Isn't that enough? Does it matter that the rest of America thinks he's a stereotypical wimpy Asian nerd? That's his problem; that's America's problem. Don't blame the women for the way in which America has accepted us and forced us to anchor the news in every major city."

"Raymond won't carry a camera when he's on vacation because he thinks people will think he's a Japanese tourist. He makes me carry the camera."

"Guilty! Guilty! Guilty!" Brenda pounded her fist on the art auction catalog like a gavel.

"Jimmy Chan says he likes Asian women because they don't get old-looking like white women."

"Guilty! Guilty! Guilty!"

Aurora sighed. "Are we any further ahead for having this discussion?"

Brenda sighed. "When I was little, kids would come up to me and say, 'Say something in Japanese.' I would resist because I didn't want to be different. Then they would say I was lucky to know another language, and I'd feel ashamed for not having obliged them."

"I always used my middle name when I got to high school. I'd write 'Aurora Reiko Crane' in the upper-right-hand corner of every page of my homework. It gave me an identity."

DURING THE AUCTION, Glenn Tompkins moved from his table and wedged an empty chair between Aurora and Brenda. Jimmy sat on the other side of Brenda, and when his duties at the auction allowed him, Raymond sat next to Aurora. Had Aurora and Brenda been students of military strategy, they would have noticed that their dinner table seating and pairing probably violated every basic rule set forth in *The Art of War* surrounded by the enemy in the low-lands, with sheer cliffs on either side.

Glenn explained every piece of Asian art that was auctioned. Brenda placed at least one bid on each item Glenn said wasn't a "good example of the form." She said that she felt sorry for the form. She ended up with a *sumi* scroll painting of a row of squat Japanese fishermen. Jimmy Chan turned and looked at the name tag on her chest one too many times, but Brenda merely put on her black shawl. Even Raymond admired her tolerance. Glenn bought a set of hand-carved miniature Japanese figurines.

"*Netsukes*," he said to Brenda as if Brenda didn't know. Aurora reminded herself to ask her later if she did.

Aurora and Raymond spoke to each other as if everyone in the room knew they had broken up and each and every one of them were listening in on their strained conversation. Raymond felt as if he and Aurora were once again sitting on a piano bench at a party where they were the only two Asians.

"Aren't you going to bid on anything?" Raymond asked.

"I like the Korean *tonsu*."

Glenn interrupted. "It's not a good example and it's probably overpriced. The drawers stick a little, and there's no key for the lock."

Fuck you, Glenn, Aurora and Raymond thought, at the same time. Aurora bid the *tonsu* up to eight hundred fifty dollars before giving it up to a professor's wife from the college. Raymond watched her bid in silence. She seemed distracted and impatient. Raymond knew he was the cause of her mood. It was too soon. He was too close. They spoke as if they were trying to rehearse each of their lines.

"How's your apartment?"

"Fine. How's the old apartment?"

"The same things need fixing." *Don't offer to fix them.*

I should offer to fix them. "Oh."

"How's work?"

"Is that a new dress?"

"Do you like it?"

There were no answers.

When it was Raymond's turn to be auctioneer, the bid stalled at a hundred dollars for two framed Aurora Crane photos of a group of children picketing the White House. Raymond bid two hundred, stunning himself and everyone else with his much too public pain. To deflect his friend's embarrassment, Jimmy bid two hundred dollars on the next piece of art, a sixth grader's collage of colored macaroni in the shape of a black fist and the words "Power to the People." For the cause.

THAT NIGHT, Aurora couldn't sleep. Unanswered questions were keeping her awake. She called Raymond.

"Raymond, is there a difference between the way an Asian woman makes love and the way a white woman makes love?"

"What kind of question is that?" Raymond stalled for time. "What about the difference between Asian and white men?"

"Men," Aurora said with disgust. "You always ask a question when you don't want to answer one. You're my only Asian lover." Too late, she realized she should have said *were*.

Raymond pondered the question. If he said yes, would it make him a racist? Yes. "What do you mean, Ro? I mean, every woman is different."

"I mean *different*, not different."

"Aurora, you want me to talk about sex with you even though we're not lovers anymore, is that it? Don't you think that's cruel?"

"I'm curious, Raymond. If you don't want to talk . . ."

There was a long silence. Raymond tried to separate what he

knew about making love with Aurora from her question. He tried to think of someone else.

There was Gretchen, the attorney, who was the first one after his divorce from Darleen. He had met her that first Christmas when he was rehired by the Orange County Department of Human Rights as a temporary replacement for a woman on maternity leave. In some ways it made sense that Gretchen was his first girlfriend after his divorce, because she had been an associate at Sylvia Beacon-Yamaki's office when Raymond was going through the divorce. Gretchen was blond and had the kind of looks people have seen somewhere before but can't place—a magazine ad, a television commercial.

She reintroduced herself by asking, "How's the single life?"

Raymond had looked almost immediately wounded by the comment, and Gretchen realized she had overstepped the bounds of confidentiality just by acknowledging the case. As they spoke, she realized that Raymond was slightly defensive about her knowing the details of his divorce. Gretchen had read his file, his résumé, his bank account statements, his community property lists, and details about his ex-wife's family. She was fascinated by the amount of material in the file that explained Chinese traditions and by how often Raymond and Darleen had referred to parents, uncles, aunts, and siblings. Two kingdoms had divorced, not just two people who fell out of love. Gretchen knew too much to ask simple questions about work, life, and the past, but Raymond had looked like he wanted to protect some anonymity, make small talk, or perhaps lie a little. She didn't know that when he spoke to her he felt a wave of shame fall over him because he still harbored an identity as a failed Chinese son. She suddenly felt bad about imposing, about being a beautiful woman who asks a painful question of a wounded man.

"I haven't eaten any Chinese food for three months; it reminds me of my ex-wife," Raymond had replied.

In the guilty and defensive silence, Gretchen asked, "Would you like to go Christmas shopping with me?"

She took him shopping and, as it turned out, brought him back into the outside world, but Raymond couldn't adjust to the way he saw himself after years of isolation in Darleen's family. As an investigator for the Department of Human Rights, he investigated and interrogated himself and guarded his sense of place and race. He found himself in violation.

Men at airports and in hotels would come right up to Gretchen as if Raymond weren't there and start talking with her or offer to help her with her bags. They assumed Raymond was (a) not with her; (b) a business partner; (c) an employee of the hotel; (d) a driver delivering her to the airport, and/or (e) someone named Hop Sing. Get back to the kitchen. Those who didn't approach her would stare at her, openly flirt with her, or say something crude, and Raymond would either have to pretend he didn't hear them or have Gretchen restrain him. Gretchen had tried to mollify Raymond by saying that men did that sort of thing to her all the time. She didn't go to war over their ignorance; why should Raymond?

"I'm no threat to them," he once said to her. "This thing between you and me couldn't be anything real. They've seen houseboys like me on television. By not standing up to them, I prove them right—Asian men are wimps."

"You don't have to prove anything to me. I know who you are. Believe me, Raymond, men's IQ's go way down when they see blond hair. It's not you."

"Yeah, like when they open the door for you and follow you through, while I'm left on the outside."

"That's happened only six or seven times. You know I'm always holding your hand and acting affectionate in public. It's not like I pretend I'm not with you. Plus don't you notice that when I'm with you these white women think they can come up to you and start talking with you? They're racist too. I've had friends ask me what it's like having a Chinese lover. You think I don't know anything about racism because I'm white—not one of those white girls you see walking around Chinatown in their black kung fu shoes, eating vegetables their Midwest mothers never heard of, wearing silk Chinese jackets, and speaking Cantonese phrases to the store clerks. You Chinese boys should be ashamed of yourselves for chasing after and seducing those ninnies, like your friend who recited phrases from the I Ching to his date over dinner at the Lotus Pod restaurant."

Gretchen had said Raymond was too sensitive. What she left unsaid was that his trying to prove something about how men reacted to her also meant trying to prove something about dating a white woman in the first place. Gretchen knew Raymond took real pride in being *able* to date her. He knew other Asian men would be envious. She was used to it and didn't really mind. She was not interested in going out with some white guy with a red Camaro who played Hacky Sack and wore Blublockers and deck shoes with no socks.

Yet Raymond had found it hard to return Gretchen's displays of affection in public. One time they had been holding hands while walking down the street and he had seen an Asian woman walking toward them about a block away. Pretending he had an itch, he had dropped Gretchen's hand, not out of guilt but to steel himself against what the woman might think, how she would look at him. He had envisioned a photo of himself in place of the definition for "double standard" in the dictionary.

"HOW ABOUT ME, Raymond?" Aurora was saying. "Was I different from one of your white lovers? Do you approach making love with me differently?"

He wanted to be honest and describe making love with Gretchen, but couldn't bring himself to answer Aurora's question even though she was pushing him to say something specific. Should he say that he had liked looking at the fine blond hairs just on the surface of Gretchen's skin? That, while making love, he probably touched her in the same way he touched Aurora? That he liked removing her business suit in the evening, her silk blouse, her pearls, her barrettes? That when her hair darkened, he had asked her to lighten it? That they both knew their relationship was temporary and that Gretchen, years later, had sent him a postcard saying that she had met someone that she liked as much as she liked Raymond?

"Oh, shit. I'm in love with you, Aurora. It's always different having sex with someone you're in love with rather than just having sex. I mean *was*. Whatever."

"Raymond, you're good at talking about race and college admissions. I want to know what you think about race and sex. I know the difference between sex and love. I'm asking you what you think. I'm not trying to torture you or interrogate you. I'm not asking you to name names."

"OK, OK. Let's rephrase the question or talk about it in parts. Maybe you're asking, when I'm making love with a white woman am I reminded or am I conscious that I'm an Asian man making love to a white woman. Or maybe you're asking, when I'm making love to a white woman am I a different lover, perhaps more vocal, more, ah, creative, adventuresome, inventive, experimental. Do white women want different things in bed from Asian women? More oral sex, less oral sex? More foreplay, less foreplay? Stop me, Ro, when you hear the right category."

"You're irritated, aren't you? What if I were a guy asking you these questions? Wouldn't you try to answer? Let's put it this way, Raymond—do you have a preference?"

Do you mean, for you as a white woman or you as an Asian woman, Raymond was tempted to ask, but he restrained himself.

"Do you really want to talk about this?"

"Yes, Raymond. Just pretend I'm a dumb guy asking a dumb question. Begin anywhere you want."

"Well, I've slept with both Asian women and white women—"

"Raymond—"

Could Raymond say it the same way he felt it? He didn't know. Could he really separate what he felt for Aurora from his answer? No. He tried to screen out what he shouldn't mention. Oral sex? Maybe. Smells? Definitely.

"What the hell, Ro. Let's get into it. Ask me a question."

"I did."

"Oh, yes. Is there a difference? Well—"

"Let's begin with yes or no, Raymond."

"Well, there's yes and no." There was a sound of aggravation at the other end of the line. "All right, let's take yes first, but I'm limited to what I know from my experience."

"What a shame," Aurora said.

Raymond was reassured by her humor. "When I first started having sex, it was mostly with white girls, because they were the only ones I knew, so I think it was different from now because we're talking about that whole period of just discovering sex and—"

"Raymond, let's skip the history. As you recall, I have the same history. Which do you prefer now?"

"Asian women."

"Why?"

"There's less explaining. There's a common bond."

"Is it just race?"

"No. I don't try to talk to a woman just because she's the only Asian in the room." There was a pause on the line as they both remembered how they had met. "I'm not talking about having to explain not coming from China and talking about Asian things and all. I'm just talking about not having to *explain*."

"I know what you mean."

"You know what I mean."

"Where do we go from here?"

"Is there a difference in bed?"

"Same thing. I don't have to explain."

"I don't know what you mean."

"You *do* know what I mean."

"Maybe *explain* isn't the right word. Maybe it has more to do with rationalization and justification."

"Then it does have something to do with race."

"Yes, I guess it does."

"I remember," Aurora said after a long pause, "the first time I massaged and scrubbed your back in the tub. You said, 'You don't have to do that.' I said, 'It's not very politically correct, is it?' You loved the image as well as the feeling, in spite of yourself. I remember saying, 'Raymond, it's OK, we're both Asian.'"

"Warning: Massage done by professional Asians. Don't try this at home with white guys."

Neither of them laughed. It was a comment Raymond had made many times before, and the familiarity hurt. He wanted to say how much he loved talking to Aurora, but instead he played the academic. "Maybe Asian women feel this race difference more than men. You can't get it out of your mind that the white guy you're in bed with can't get it out of his mind that he's sleeping with an Asian woman, and that might have something to do with the attraction."

"You're talking about fear."

"Fear of the big slip of the tongue? That he'll eventually say something racist?"

"Brenda says Asian men fall back on the racism thing because they don't want to talk about comparing cock size."

"Brenda can—"

"When you first slept with an Asian woman, wasn't it a big deal to you?"

"Yes."

"What did it feel like? What were you thinking?"

"I was very happy."

"A sense of belonging?"

"A sense of belonging. When we walked down the street, people thought we were beautiful together. I thought so too. I didn't know it was supposed to feel like that. I think it was more than 'Look at that cute Chinese couple.' Perhaps it was obvious how much we were in love. Old women in Chinatown would smile at us. One of the vendors along Stockton Street gave us a bar of sandalwood soap."

"Were you trying to prove something to yourself, to your family?"

"No, I don't think so. Maybe I was. The nonacceptance of my white girlfriends was always an issue."

"Did your father like your Chinese girlfriend?"

"He adored her. He adores you too."

There was a pause. Both of them began to say something but stopped.

"Next question, Ro."

"I don't know whether I understand what you're saying. Maybe I understand too well. Didn't that wonderful feeling you talk about ever happen with a white girl?"

"I remember going camping with my college girlfriend. A woman camping next to us walked over and gave us some cake she had made and commented that we looked like we were having fun. She said my girlfriend's curly blond hair was gorgeous and that we looked cute together. My impulse was to be wary, but there was nothing in the woman's voice to suggest that she meant anything other than what she said. I took a picture of my girlfriend right after that, sitting by my old Volkswagen with her dog. She was luminous."

"The woman made you feel like you belonged with your girl-friend and it didn't have anything to do with race."

"Yes."

"Is it an issue with us?"

"I don't know; is it?"

"It was in the beginning, but now I'm not so sure."

"Can you really say there's a race consciousness one minute but not the next?"

"Was I attracted to you because it's *easier* for me or because it's easier for society?"

"Society already accepts you, Ro. You can be with anyone and it's acceptable, in any society, anywhere."

"Brenda says you only go out with Asian women now because you're too politically correct to do anything else and you have a job that's too politically correct for you to have a flaw like a white wife."

"Are you sure Brenda isn't calling me and not you?"

"She says it's either that or you have an inferiority complex about dating white women, but I told her that certainly wasn't true."

"Thanks for standing up for me."

"Brenda is not all stupid, Raymond."

"What you just said sounds pretty stupid."

"She asked me why was it that, with all the white women you've slept with, you're always their first Asian lover—"

"Shit, Brenda can—"

"Let me finish. *And*, with all the Asian women you've slept with, you're *their* first Asian lover? Brenda called it 'racial deflowering.' Pretty funny, huh?"

"Brenda should talk."

"Don't attack Brenda until you answer."

"'All the women I've slept with' is a gross exaggeration."

"OK—*many?*"

"You two make me out to be some kind of racial plunderer."

"An affirmative action Hun."

"Brenda's term?"

"Yes." Aurora laughed.

If she laughs, Raymond thought, *I don't have to answer.* He didn't have a good answer anyway. Brenda was nearly right. What was he trying to prove? He remembered fantasies he'd had about Brenda's body.

Aurora stopped laughing. "Men don't think they really know a woman until they sleep with her. Brenda knows men, and she says she knows you. She doesn't have to sleep with you to know you."

Raymond retreated. "So what do you want to know?"

"I'm sorry, Raymond, I'm not trying to be mean. I just want you to answer my question. What's the difference between making love with a white woman and making love with an Asian woman? You don't have to get clinical or autobiographical. Just give me your impression."

Raymond was about to ask if Aurora was planning on sleeping with women next, but it was time to get the interrogation over with. He confessed.

"I'm always surprised at how much Asian women enjoy sex."

"Now you're being honest—" Suddenly Aurora didn't want to hear any more. She didn't want to know any more. She knew Raymond didn't want to say any more.

"Raymond?"

"What?"

"When do you see me being Japanese?"

"When you tell me about your mother. There are things she does that are very Japanese. You do them too."

She wanted to be reminded what they were, but it was too intimate a request.

7   moment resistance

RAYMOND SHOUTED HELLO AND ENTERED HIS FATHER'S house in one motion. He found Wood at work in his study.

"Hey, son, you got any furniture yet?" he asked, without looking up from the blueprints on his drafting table.

Raymond shook his head. "I've been busy."

His father pointed at the framed black-and-white photo of himself, Raymond, and Aurora standing in the silver mist of a waterfall at Yosemite. "You ought to apologize and stick with her. She takes nice pictures. She's a pretty girl. You're a lucky boy." He picked up the photo as if he picked it up every day. He shook his head. Wood adored Aurora. She got him to do things old Chinese men didn't do. Go hiking in Yosemite. Go to Lake Tahoe and Reno and be within minutes of gambling casinos yet not go gambling. Kiss her on the cheek in greeting.

"I didn't do anything wrong to have to apologize." Raymond resented the implication. "It's just over and has been over for months." He turned to leave the room.

His father looked up, placing a paperweight on the curled ends of a roll of blueprints. "You'll find a new girlfriend."

Raymond turned to leave the room again. "I just came by to see how you're doing, Pop."

"What does the word 'redundant' mean to you?"

Raymond turned again. Engineers of his father's generation had difficulty with spelling. "It means to say or write the same thing over and over."

"Am I redundant?"

"Sometimes."

Wood stuck the tip of his pencil in the electric pencil sharpener and motioned for him to come to the desk. "Look at these building plans. I want to show you something." He lifted the paperweight and rolled a couple of the blueprints over. He pointed at the side view of a large building. "See these beams all along the side of the building?"

Raymond told himself that patience was a virtue.

"Structural redundancy in a building is a good thing. The more redundancy, the stronger the building."

Raymond sucked air through his teeth. "Yeah, I get it, Dad. If I marry someone Chinese I'll have structural redundancy. It'll make the relationship stronger. We'll use the same genetic building materials, and our children will come out pure and strong. Dad, I was married to a structurally redundant woman once already. I had Chinese structural beams all around me, and the building collapsed."

"You have too much education, Smart Mouth." Wood pointed his pencil at Raymond. "I was going to say that you and Aurora have structural redundancy."

"She doesn't realize it."

"No, she realizes it. You don't have to remind her of it all the time."

"I don't—"

"When you were married to Darleen, did you ever introduce her as your Chinese wife?"

There was a long silence between them.

"What else are you working on?" Raymond asked.

"Something called 'moment resistance.'" Wood turned back to his blueprints. "I read this book that says one out of every four people on this earth is Chinese. There are a billion Chinese in China, and at least five hundred million of them are women."

"Yeah, Dad. Mao said women hold up half the sky." Raymond looked through the pile of unopened mail on the corner of the table.

"Exactly." His father paused.

"Exactly what, Dad?"

"Women." Wood paused again, then moved from his blueprints to the computer table.

"Women what, Dad?"

"I'm going there to find a wife." Wood moved the mouse along the mouse pad, then opened a file. A three-dimensional drawing of a building appeared.

"For me?"

"Don't be so self-centered, son." Wood paused. "You could come with me. I'm going to find a wife. You can help me pick her out. She'd be your stepmother, after all."

"A wife in China? You've never been to China!" Raymond took a deep breath, then laughed. "Oh, I get it, Dad. It's a joke. You're just trying to cheer me up. Get me one of those nice country girls, have babies, grow veggies on the side of the house. Someone who can order food fluently in a Chinese restaurant so I don't have to use my broken Cantonese."

"I'm serious, son."

Still suspicious, Raymond waited for the punch line.

"I need a wife. I need to be married. I'm kind of lonely, you know, especially with you gone." Another silence, his father's serious silence and Raymond's guilty silence blended together. "But," his father continued, "you've given me an idea. If we married two sisters, we'd have only one mother-in-law to deal with."

That was the punch line, but it wasn't a joke. Raymond could hardly recognize his father's voice, it was so edged with enthusiasm. He chatted on about travel agents and sending letters through relatives and his friends' relatives. Raymond listened in stunned amazement. Practical, sensible structural engineers did not talk like this. Besides, his father seemed like too much of an American to marry someone from China. At the moment, he was dressed like a fraternity boy, in a dark-green polo shirt, khaki pants, and brown loafers with little leather tassels. But Raymond thought again, and conceded that an American looking for a wife in China should look American. Perhaps he should throw in a monogrammed sweater and a golf club for good measure.

What would his father talk about with a Chinese wife from China? If he married someone who spoke only Mandarin, he wouldn't be able to converse with her in his Americanized second-generation Cantonese. Raymond tired at the thought of having to explain every trivial piece of information to someone from another country. Perhaps that was the root of his problems: he couldn't commit to family responsibility of that magnitude. He wondered whether his father would try to palm off on him the job of teaching his new wife the basics. What were the basics? *"See Dick run. Run Dick run." I don't think so.* He tried to picture himself as some kind of cultural flight attendant, who would say to his new stepmother, "Pull the card from the seat back in front of you and follow along with me. There are no walk-ups at a drive-up window. If you're Chinese it's OK to double-park in Chinatown. As a boy, I was in love with Annette Funicello. Bicycles in America have twenty-one speeds. In case of an emergency, dial 911."

It had been a long time since he had heard his father make plans. Their dinners together had the familiar uneasy tension that went with eating in silence. Food was a kind of conversation. His father pushed food toward him with his chopsticks and urged

Raymond to eat with a wave of the chopsticks over the food. More winter melon soup meant: "Glad to see you again; let's not try to talk personal talk." Raymond no longer complimented his father on his cooking; he had sensed that his father felt patronized by such comments. When they did talk now, their remarks centered around the television, which his father had moved near the dinner table. Beside it he had placed a large wooden statue of the rotund and smiling god Hotai.

"Uncle Ted's son had his pick of pretty girls in the ancestral village."

Raymond tried to remember Uncle Ted's son, but all he could come up with was a scrawny ten-year-old with fingerprints on his thick glasses, playing with his toy microscope. Then he remembered that they had met in Berkeley when Raymond was in graduate school and Stevie was an undergraduate nerd with a slide rule, on his way to becoming a nerd of a nuclear engineer.

"You should see her, son. Looks like a Chinese Sophia Loren. She's already pregnant."

The only picture Raymond could conjure up was of Little Stevie dressed in striped bell-bottoms and a plaid shirt, a rolled-up comic book in his back pocket, seated on some throne reserved for Chinese boys with big blue American passports, while the procession of village girls paraded in front of him—the Chinese Sophia Loren, the Chinese Ann-Margret, the Chinese Annette Funicello— all of them waving Mao's little red book. Little Stevie pointed at the Chinese Sophia Loren, soaking wet in a white cotton dress that stuck to her body like Saran Wrap. Each of her gorgeous breasts was bigger than Little Stevie's face. She walked toward him, saved from spending the rest of her life diving for sponges or oysters or whatever lived at the bottom of the ocean in China. Little Stevie showed her pictures of his pink Thunderbird, the satellite dish perched on the roof of his split-level home, a McDonald's Happy Meal. A deal was struck. He gave her family a case of American toilet paper. There was a gasp from the assembled villagers, then cheering.

"My phone's already been ringing," Raymond's father said. A Filipino nursing student with two months left on her student visa had appeared at his doorstep in full dress whites. Photos of Chinese women from his ancestral village had begun to arrive. He spread them out on the drafting table and adjusted the lamp. "Tell me what you think."

What was Raymond supposed to look for? Bone structure? Large peasant feet? A strong back? How was he supposed to talk to his father about available women? Bodacious tits, Dad. Nice ass.

"Wait a minute, Dad. You're telling me you're going to pick someone by mail? Like a picture bride?"

"No, it's not the old days anymore. I'm going over there and pick her out." Wood moved the photos from the middle of the drafting table to the edge closest to Raymond, as if they had some kind of gravitational pull that would draw Raymond to them.

"How does it work?"

"A matchmaker sets it up. They send photos and we send photos. Then we narrow it down, check the families, birth dates, superstitious Chinese stuff, and make the trip."

"You mean they check your American passport, how big your house is, how big your bank account is."

"It's an opportunity for both of us." His father gestured toward the photos. "Just look."

Raymond's ego was piqued. He imagined the fresh-faced, rosy-cheeked, ponytailed gifts on the cover of *China Reconstructs*, in their starched school uniforms, parading in front of him with the red flags of the People's Republic waving in the background, the cheering of a million workers. Prodigal American son comes home. The ultimate filial obligation.

"It's a meat market, Dad. It's disgusting."

"It's reality and opportunity."

"Their reality; our fantasy."

"I'm too old for fantasy. I just want a wife."

"More children?"

"There's a heritage to protect. The family tree."

"Are you forgetting about me?"

"A Chinese girl won't have your modern ideas of marriage."

"How old are these 'girls,' Dad?"

"I need some photos to send to China. Will you ask Aurora to take them?"

"I have a camera, Dad."

Raymond edged closer to the photos. He wanted to say to his father that these were the wrong reasons to get married. He wished he could remember what his father and mother had been like as a young couple in love. If he could, would he understand what his father wanted?

Raymond remembered his mother once called his father "my pumpkin." It was probably the hippest, most American thing Helen had ever said. The turn of events that led up to this utterance were curious. The family had driven down to Carmel for the day. Along the way, a man driving in the next lane had made a sudden lane change, forcing his father onto the shoulder. His father gunned the engine, pulled alongside the other car, and gave the other driver the finger. The other driver pulled in front again and slammed on the brakes, forcing them to skid to a stop. He jumped out of his car and ran back toward theirs, screaming, "Goddamn Chink driver." Raymond's father screamed back a string of obscenities Raymond had never heard him use before. He had his door open and was struggling to get out, but Helen had locked her arms around her husband's neck to keep him inside the car. The other man lost his nerve and ran back to his own car. Wood beat on the steering wheel. Helen wept, still clutching his neck in a death grip. Raymond jumped up and down on the back seat, laughing, punching the air, and yelling, "Fight! Fight!" as if he were in a schoolyard.

That weekend the weather was beautiful, and Raymond's father and mother decided on a whim they should spend the weekend in Carmel. *On a whim* was not something Chinese parents did. No extra clothes, no toothbrushes, no shaving kit. They had to buy everything—swimming trunks, T-shirts, socks, beach sandals, a sun hat, a new bathing suit Raymond's mother had seen in *Vogue*. Out on the Seventeen Mile Drive, with the smell of the ocean in the air, Wood rubbed his four o'clock shadow and said to Helen, "Maybe I just won't shave this weekend." That was when she called him "my pumpkin." They held hands. They ate American food. On the way home, they bought their first artichokes, in "The Artichoke Capital of the World."

Raymond was about the same age now as his father was when they stayed in Carmel *on a whim*. He was trying to determine whether his father's desire to marry a Chinese woman/girl he had never met, from a Chinese village he had never been to, was just a whim. *I'm the son—I'm supposed to be the one doing things on a whim*, Raymond thought.

The phone rang. When his father answered it, Raymond picked up the photos of the women, walked into the living room, and sat on the sofa as if he planned to interview each one. They were all young. From the living room he listened to his father and wondered if his father's heart could stand being broken again.

Raymond refused to ask Aurora to take his father's picture, but in the end he agreed to do it himself. The viewfinder on the camera helped him to narrow his view. It made Raymond's father and his desires more two-dimensional and excluded Raymond from the picture. The more photos he took of his father, the more clearly he saw his point of view. The look in his father's face each time he snapped another photo said to Raymond, "Support my mission; frame my future."

In the first roll of film, Raymond positioned his father with landmarks in the background—the Golden Gate Bridge, Coit Tower, a mansion they didn't live in, next to a Porsche, a Mercedes-Benz. He was dressed in a suit in all of them. By the time they had finished the second roll of film, Raymond wanted his father to look younger, stronger, richer, happier, and more heroic. He drove his father to a vintage clothing store and picked out a whole new wardrobe for him. He posed him in the scenes he remembered from the family album, the ones his mother took— Dad in an aloha shirt just after the war, army pay in hand, a big band, a dance floor. "Hey, Dad, stand by that old car. We had one just like it, remember?" Raymond got his father telling stories he'd heard dozens of times. When Wood got to the punch line, he'd snap the photo.

Slowly, frame by frame, they relived a past, were father and son, army buddies, schoolmates, coworkers. They double-dated, bought cigarettes from the cigarette girl, paid fifteen cents a gallon for gas, bought a Buick (because it looked different from a Chevrolet), wore heavy dress shoes with spit shines and metal taps. They had girl-friends, met Helen all over again, marveled in unison, "That Helen, what a woman!" A wolf whistle. The photos put their mourning for her behind them, brought a common past forward. In the last photo, Raymond balanced the camera on the fender of a car, set the timer, and ran to his father's side, putting his arm around his neck and pretending to choke a laugh out of him. It was the heyday, the good ol' days, the way it was.

◆ ◆ ◆

LATER, ALONE IN HIS FATHER'S HOUSE, Raymond pulled an engineering manual from the bookshelf and looked up the definition of "moment resistance":

"Moment resistance—structural rigidity and flexibility, as in the ability of a window frame to withstand sudden shock or stress without the glass shattering."

Moment resistance, Raymond thought. *Structural rigidity and flexibility. As in the ability of a couple to withstand sudden shock—the death of a child, infidelity, a serious illness, periods of silence, separations, a brief rage—or to flex without the relationship shattering.*

When Aurora called Raymond and told him she was going home, he didn't grasp what she meant. She said it without explanation, then paused, as if waiting for his reaction. He thought about all the ways they had used the word "home" and heard it now as a measure of her unhappiness with him, of her determination to separate herself from him. He thought about the other ways they had used the word "home." Finally Aurora explained that her father was selling Aurora Auto Parts and retiring. She was going back to Minneapolis for the party. She asked Raymond to water her plants and pick up the mail. He wondered if he should be insulted or compliant.

"I don't have a key," he said.

"I'll leave a key with the manager." Even over the phone, she could feel him soften. She was respecting his pride. "I'll tell him you forgot them. You've done that before."

"How long will you be gone?"

"Two weeks."

"You have problems being with your parents for more than five days straight."

"My sister will be there."

"You haven't been home in a while," he said, trying not to sound as if he were interrogating her.

"My father's giving me one of the store's little delivery trucks. I'm driving back."

Raymond wanted to comment on her poor driving but resisted.

"It'll be OK. I'll be careful. I'll call you," she said hurriedly, as if she were answering his unasked questions.

"The Badlands are nice," he said. He knew how lame that sounded, but he couldn't stop himself. He knew being in the apartment would torment him. He wanted to ask if accepting cruelty was proof of friendship.

"I've got to go down to Macy's and pick out a dress for the retirement party." She paused, wondering if she should make the invitation explicit. "Do you want to help me? I'll bring your key." Immediately she regretted asking.

Raymond said yes, twice. He immediately regretted the second yes.

If she was cruel, then he was a masochist. If Aurora was Hoss Cartwright, he was Hop Sing. He would rather play houseboy than nothing at all.

HE SPOTTED AURORA in the women's wear section that had for its theme something along the lines of "party dresses for young women in college sororities who read a lot of fashion magazines." Even from a distance Raymond could tell there wasn't a single dress on the racks suitable for her. She stood before a mirror, holding a drop-waist dress against her, not the right dress for a woman with such long legs. As he drew near he caught her eye in the mirror and was relieved to see relief in her eyes. A saleswoman asked him if he needed help.

"He's with me," Aurora said.

"I'm with her," Raymond wanted to say, but he refrained.

"My mother says I can't wear black. 'It's a retirement party, not a funeral.'" She hung the dress on a hook beside the mirror but didn't turn around. She was wearing black jeans and a plain white T-shirt. She suddenly looked very young.

"Prints don't look good on you." Raymond wanted to touch her, but he knew he couldn't. "You look good in olive green. What's your mother wearing?"

"Floral print." Aurora frowned.

"You wouldn't want to clash with her."

"I don't know." Aurora moved to another rack.

"There's nothing here. Let's go to Union Street and find something that doesn't look so department store-ish."

"I don't have much time."

"I saw something there the other day that would look good on you." He touched her arm, then held her elbow in his palm and steered her toward the elevator.

JULIA SHOWED UP AT THE AIRPORT in a Jeep Wrangler that looked as clean as the day it was bought. When Aurora caught sight of her, her first thought was that Julia looked more Asian. Was it that her face had matured, or was it simply that Aurora had been around more Asians lately?

"How's Mom?" Aurora said, beginning to gauge tactics and strategies.

"Mom's Mom," Julia said. "In our next life, I move away from home and you stay."

"You can leave."

It was an old argument.

"While you're visiting, Mom wants me to stay at home, sleep in our old room. I told her I have to take care of my cat. She says I should have Miles take care of the cat. 'He's always there anyway.'" Julia's imitation of her mother was better than Aurora's.

"Who won?"

Julia gave Aurora their mother's look. "We get to play Mom's fantasy family for the next five days," Julia sighed. "At least I'm allowed to go to work."

"Dad?"

"Dad's great. He and all the regulars have been drinking champagne at the shop. The Snap-on Tool rep gave him three engraved gold-plated wrenches in a felt-lined wooden box. The first wrench reads, 'Hank, don't take no shit.' The second one reads, 'Hank, don't give no shit.' And the last one says, 'Hank, you ain't in the shit business no more.' So Dad had that printed on some gold oil filters, and he's passing them out to his favorite customers. The Mac Tool rep gave him an autographed babe calendar that says, 'Sock(et) Tool me, Big Hank!' There's a poster down in the basement that reads, 'Swing your big Crane my way, Hank Crane! Love ya, Jessica.' He's the center of attention."

"Takes the heat off us. Let's go by there and surprise him."

"Dad would love to show you off, but we can't. Mom wants us home to fold cranes and do party favors."

"I guess gold oil filters aren't her idea of honoring all those years of hard work."

"Yeah."

Julia pulled off the freeway and took the scenic route home, the way their school bus used to go. It was not very scenic, but it took longer. For a while there was only the steady hum of the Jeep's tires on the pavement.

"So, as Dad says, how's that Chinaman shack job of yours?"

Aurora watched the houses pass by and tried to remember who lived in them. "Raymond and I broke up." She kept the story simple for now. She assured Julia she was being vague only because the situation was vague. "He still comes over," she said, then remembered that "over" was sisterly shorthand for "stays overnight." She didn't correct herself or elaborate. The details could wait.

"You seeing someone else?"

Aurora nodded, which Julia knew meant it wasn't serious.

"If I'm going to be with an old guy, I'd rather have Eric Clapton," said Julia. "There's an old guy worth two barrettes." "Two barrettes" was code for "It takes two barrettes to keep your hair in place when you fuck him."

"God, you always had the hots for Eric."

"He looks better now."

"Asian men in their forties want us to act like Elvira Madigan trapped in the screenplay for 9 1/2 *Weeks* with the Chinese guy from *The Lover* in the Mickey Rourke role."

"Who's Elvira Madigan?"

Apropos of nothing, Aurora said, "Miles isn't white."

"Miles has white values. He can't help it. His father is a dentist and he went to Pepperdine College in Malibu. Christ, we play on a volleyball team. He wants to get a golden retriever and some golf clubs." Julia stopped at a stop sign and turned to Aurora. "You know what was wrong with Raymond?" Aurora didn't answer. "Whenever I saw him reading, he was always holding a pen in his hand. The guy should read a book now and then that he can find at the supermarket. Does he still talk about the sixties?" A car behind them honked.

Aurora shrugged.

"Oh, man. Living in the past and having a midlife-going-bald crisis. It's only a few years from that to a dishonest haircut—you know, the sweep-the-few-remaining-strands-over-the-top do. Then they buy a red Corvette because their penis doesn't work anymore. I couldn't live with that."

"He's not going bald."

"Stand by your man."

Julia pulled into their parents' driveway.

"Don't tell them about Raymond and me. I don't want to hear 'I told you so.'"

"Well, Ro, if things go according to normal, we won't be discussing Ray and Miles at all."

NORMA WAS HAPPY to have both her daughters home. All afternoon the three of them folded origami cranes and strung them together or set them aside to give away. Julia had the best handwriting, so she got stuck writing name cards for the dinner tables.

"Why can't I write their nicknames?" she said. "Nobody calls Larry Haugen 'Larry'; they all call him 'Fly Trap,' as in 'Shut your fly trap for a change.' And then there's Mac, and Hippo, and Ace, and Swede, and Beaver."

"How's Ricky Little?" Aurora asked. They both burst out laughing.

"Richard's last name isn't Little," Norma said. "It's Leitel."

Julia and Aurora tried to suppress their laughter.

"It's something dirty, isn't it?" Their mother shook her head. "I warned your father about talking like that in front of you girls."

The next two days were pleasant. The day before the party, Julia and Aurora rummaged through the closets and staged a fashion show in their old bedroom. They planned to sneak out later in Hank's Cadillac and meet Miles for drinks and tiramisù.

"Did I really wear my skirts this short?" Aurora asked.

Like the voice-over in a horror movie trailer, Julia announced, "It came back from the dead. It was chartreuse. It was short. It had a white plastic belt. It showed your thighs!" She screamed in terror.

Aurora held up a pair of black stockings. "Fishnet is back."

"Not in Minneapolis." Julia sat down on her old bed. The masking tape that divided her side of the room from Aurora's was long gone. "In fact, the color black only recently arrived here."

Aurora slipped out of the skirt and pulled on an orange polyester A-line dress with an oval cutout just below the neckline. "So how are you and Miles getting along?"

"I think he wants to get married."

The announcement called for expressions of delight and support, but Aurora and Julia fell silent, mulling over the implications.

"Mom and Dad?"

"They don't know."

"When?"

"I'm hoping it's just one of Miles's phases. He thinks time is running out."

"You don't want to get married?"

"Dad will have a heart attack. Besides, how can I marry someone who he doesn't believe exists?"

"That bad, huh?"

"You'd think all the racist shit he and Mom went through would have made him more open-minded."

"'I want better for my daughters.'"

"You got that right." Julia started folding some of the clothes Aurora had tossed on her bed. "It's too exhausting to even think about."

"What does Mom think?"

"She tells Dad that it's part of growing up. I think she's hoping I'll grow out of it."

"She just calls it an it?"

"Yeah. Raymond is at least allowed a name, even though Dad thinks of him as an opium addict who's been married three times. I think by now both of us were supposed to have married white boys in Dad's image."

"Where did we go wrong?"

"That's exactly what Dad says."

Aurora rummaged through her suitcase and pulled out a pair of black tights and a black bra. "I think I'll wear this orange retro number out for drinks tonight." She slipped the dress off her shoulders and traded her white bra for the black one.

"So what was it between you and Raymond?" Julia asked.

"We were communicating too much."

"Hmm, yeah, that's a real problem. Don't you just hate when that happens?"

"No, really, Jules." Aurora examined the tights for holes. "I think Raymond needs a woman who can be a hundred percent Asian every day. Some days I got tired of it."

"I think Raymond gets tired of it too, but he won't admit it."

"You hardly know him," Aurora said defensively, but she knew there was a lot of truth to what Julia said.

"Raymond has banana tendencies, but that job of his keeps him from peeling. Or he's popcorn—you know, yellow yellow yellow yellow until you put him under pressure, then he turns white."

Aurora turned her back to Julia. "Where did you learn that stuff? Zip me up." She pulled on her black leather jacket to complete the look. "You got the keys?"

Julia nodded. "We're meeting Miles at the bar. He won't ride in the Cadillac."

"Too much of a black thang, huh?"

"It's that and he's paranoid that one of Dad's cronies will see him riding in Dad's car and call the cops."

"How's Miles going to get from that to telling Dad he wants to marry you? Quite a stretch."

Julia played with the car keys. "It's kind of sad. I think deep down Miles and I believe in each other, but there's a sense that both of us would be relieved if I just happened to find someone else who was Japanese or white or even mixed like me, or if he met a black woman. We don't say it. It's just there sometimes. He does the same thing I do: I see a pretty black woman and can imagine them together, he sees a guy who looks like me and tries to make a funny comment about it. Then he'll reach for me and hold my hand or put his arm around my waist. I think he's trying to make me feel more secure. We pretend we don't have to struggle to stay together, but neither one of us wants to confront Dad."

"Should Miles make a stand in front of Dad? You know, 'I love your daughter, Mr. Crane, and I want to marry her and take care of her for the rest of our lives.'"

"It's not fear." Julia's eyes welled up. "It's funny, I think Miles has too much respect for Dad. It's like he respects his racism. Does that make sense?"

"No, it doesn't." Aurora sat down next to Julia. "Does Dad respect Miles for hiding in the background—for respecting his racism, as you put it?"

"Dad doesn't think he's a racist."

"And?"

"And Miles should prove it?"

"Uh, no, Jules."

"Miles should decide for himself if it's really Dad that's holding him back or something else between the two of us?"

"You knew the answer, didn't you?"

"Miles doesn't want to stand between a father and his love for his daughter."

"That's an excuse. So what do you do? Wait for a more sensible ethnic pairing to show up? Someone who's as nice as Miles, but acceptable to Dad?"

Julia shook her head.

"One of you is going to have to stand up and be a man. Jules, you're a bridge between them, not a boundary."

"Is that one of Ray's sociology metaphors?"

"No, I just thought that one up myself."

"So, has Raymond found an all-Asian girl?"

Aurora shrugged.

BY THE MORNING OF THE PARTY, the reunification of the family and the general mood was beginning to show some strain. Pleased as Norma was to have her girls back under her roof, their presence reminded her that their lives were still "business as usual." She ventured into the borders of all their old arguments as if to test whether they would violate the idyllic restoration of the family by raising their voices to her, but neither took the bait. They had braced themselves for her by giving each other a high five in the morning and saying, "Let's show some *gaman*, endure *über alles*."

"Kimi's daughter is getting married in June." Translation: *I have to explain to my friends that my daughters are career girls.*

"The *Star-Tribune* just hired a Japanese American reporter." Translation: *You don't have to go to San Francisco to find work.* Second translation: *Maybe you can find an excuse to call him and he'll ask you out.* Third translation: *Julia stayed home, why can't you?*

"Why do you girls always have to wear black?" Translation: *Why do you deliberately make yourselves unattractive?* Second translation: *Be more feminine and maybe you'll get a husband.*

"How's your apartment?" Translation: (For Julia) *Has he moved in?* (For Aurora) *Are you still living in sin?* Second translation: *In our day we wouldn't even think about it.*

"Ro, I hope you'll be able to take pictures at the retirement party, or would you like someone else to do it?" Translation: *Can you take regular pictures instead of that artsy kind?*

"This party is just for your father's business friends, employees, and our friends." Translation: *Don't invite Miles.*

The party turned out to be great fun. It became an impromptu Hank Crane roast. Julia and Aurora were perfect daughters, and every man at the party complimented them, while the wives asked Aurora if she was getting married. "All you girls wait too long to have a family." They didn't ask Julia because they knew.

Six separate times during the evening someone went up to Hank and said, "How could anyone as ugly as you have such beautiful daughters?"

"Here, have a gold oil filter for your mouth—it'll filter out all that shit you dish out."

"Oh, Hank, stop it. The girls," Norma kept saying.

"ARE THEY UP?" Hank asked Norma, as he poured his morning coffee and joined her at the kitchen table.

"They're still asleep." Norma separated the paper, pulling out the sports section for Hank. "I don't think the girls are used to drinking champagne."

Hank pushed the paper away and stared at Norma in disbelief. "That ain't the half of it. Those two can drink plenty, and they can obviously damn well do anything else they please."

While Norma tried to tiptoe around sensitive subjects, protective of the illusion of family serenity, Hank worked at focusing a bright light on what he saw as two failed lives.

Norma put down her paper. "Aurora said she'd take us all out for Sunday brunch today. We can drop off her pictures of the party at that one-hour developing place on the way and pick them up after."

"Am I wrong, Norma? Did I do something wrong to deserve this?"

"Young people have their own lives these days—"

"My own daughters tell me I'm a racist. I'm not a racist. I just want better for them."

"You're not a racist, dear."

"Hell, I got nothing against nobody. In the navy, everyone was equal. I treated all the men the same."

"I know." Norma listened for signs that Aurora and Julia might be stirring.

"Hell, the girls think they know it all with this racial identity crap. You and I know prejudice and discrimination. Your whole family was uprooted and sent off to the concentration camps, and your uncle Mas and uncle Frank volunteered for the 442nd Regimental Combat Team in the war to prove their loyalty. They didn't complain and bellyache; they're real American heroes. I married you, we live next door to Germans. No one's got nothing to prove by me. Your family didn't ever say an unkind word about me. My Irish ancestors were treated like scum when they came to America. I've got nothing against Miles or that Chinaman shack job because of race. Excuse me—*Chinese* shack job. I'm on my daughters' side. They're my flesh and blood. It hurts me to see Miles and Ray using them until something better comes along. I just don't understand it. Show some pride." Hank pulled the curtain aside and gazed into the backyard.

Norma watched him in silence. They had had variations on this conversation before, sometimes with Julia and Aurora present. The arguments led to long periods of silence between Hank and his daughters. Norma didn't want this weekend to end in the same way.

Hank shook his head. "All that bullcrap about being Asian American women. They didn't have a clue until they went to college and took those ethnic studies classes. Those two are as Japanese as I am. The only Japanese word they know is *yeah-but*." He didn't laugh at his old joke. "They didn't even know about the relocation camps until Ro came home from Columbia with the news. And what happened? What happened, Norma?"

Norma gave him the answer he was waiting for. "They didn't even know I had been in the camps."

"Why?"

"Because they never asked."

"Didn't know. Never asked. Didn't matter. Brilliant. College tuition goes pretty far these days."

"Stop it, Henry," Norma said. "The girls just want to lead their lives the way they want to. We can't stop them."

"I'm not a bigot; I'm their father." Hank pushed his mug aside abruptly, spilling coffee on the table. "All I see is that I paid for their college education and now they come home with this ethnic identity crap and jokes about white guys." Hank wiped up the spill with a napkin.

"Are you finished, Henry?"

"I'm not in the shit business anymore."

"Are you finished?" Norma reached across the table and grabbed Hank's hand and gave it a squeeze. "Put on a suit for brunch. Look nice for the girls."

"I'm their father. I got a right."

"And they're your only daughters."

When they were ready to leave, Hank led Aurora out to the garage to show her the pickup truck he was giving her. It was teal green, with a matching new canopy over the bed of the truck and an automatic transmission, good for all those San Francisco hills. It looked almost brand-new.

"It's got your name on the side."

Aurora walked around to the side. Aurora Auto Parts.

"It's been detailed and tuned. I've put some extra oil in the back, some water, extra fan belts, tool kit under the seat, gold oil filters." He laughed. "We got a lot of gold oil filters left over. Tires are brand-new radials. I signed you up on our auto club card. It's in the glove compartment. The shop's insurance is still good on it for another couple of months. It's in the glove compartment. Maps are in there too, with a list of motels along the way. I'm sorry it ain't a car, but these days I hear women are buying trucks. There's a tape deck in it—"

Aurora stopped him. "It's beautiful, Dad. Thank you." She kissed him on the cheek.

"Maybe Julia should drive out to California with you."

"Julia's got to work, Dad. I'll be fine."

"You can paint over the sign later if you want."

Aurora walked to the side of the truck and touched her name. "I wouldn't do that."

This is what fathers do.

8 chinese girls

RAYMOND WAS WATERING AURORA'S PLANTS WHEN THE
buzzer rang. He pushed the talk button on the intercom.

"Who is it?"

Silence.

"Who is it?"

"Raymond?"

"Yes."

"What the fuck are you doing there?"

"Who's this?"

"Brenda."

"Brenda?"

"Where's Ro?"

"She's in Minneapolis, at her father's retirement thing."

"Oh, shit. I forgot."

"Do you want to come in?"

"You're not doing anything weird in there, are you?"

"No, Brenda."

"What are you doing up there?"

"I'm watering her plants and picking up the mail."

Silence.

"Does Ro know you're doing that?"

"Do you want to come in? It's safe."

"Sure."

Raymond steeled himself for a meeting of the minds.

Brenda was wearing a long raincoat, and all that was visible were her Lycra leggings. "You've been working out?" Raymond asked, as he closed the door behind her. He wondered what Brenda looked like in skintight Lycra.

"Yeah." Brenda scanned the apartment for signs of creepy male behavior.

"I'm almost done watering the plants." Raymond showed her the watering can. Proof. "Was Ro supposed to leave something for you?"

"No."

"Why did you come by?"

"I saw the windows open and thought I'd use her telephone."

"Don't you have one in your car?"

"Not working."

"Are you staying? You want something to drink? Take your coat?"

"No. Maybe some water."

She hugged her raincoat to her as if it were armor. Each creak in the wooden floor seemed to indicate the presence of land mines. Raymond handed her the glass and returned to watering plants. Brenda would talk if she wanted.

"Are you sure you don't want to take your coat off?" Raymond said after a minute, when Brenda showed no signs of leaving. He couldn't resist asking again, if for no other reason than to level the field of conflict.

Brenda didn't back down from challenges, and Raymond's plan to put her on the defensive backfired. She removed her raincoat. She had on a loose-fitting white tank top over a pink unitard. The sight of her took the air out of the apartment. Too late, Raymond realized that if he faltered for just one millisecond, Brenda would report him, pond-scum male pig that he was, to Aurora. Not that Brenda could help herself in front of men. The tits. The long, slim, non-*daikon* legs. She looked Raymond right in the eyes, fingering the diamond pendant at her cleavage. Her eyes said she knew she could break him. All he had to do was look. Once.

Raymond held her gaze until his eyes began to dry out. Brenda tugged at the tank top, pulling it down to cover her crotch, which only succeeded in lowering the neckline of the shirt. Raymond couldn't stand the heat and turned toward the kitchen, still grasping the watering can. The master was out, and there were chores to be done. From the next room, he heard Brenda clinking the ice cubes in her glass.

When Raymond returned to the living room, she was French-braiding her hair in front of the mirror above the fireplace, holding a hair clip in her mouth. He remembered that Brenda was twenty-nine. He loved twenty-nine-year-old women; they were actually worried about turning thirty. The insecurity about age, combined with their confidence at having begun to realize their early career ambitions, was terribly sexy. Young lawyers, young doctors, young professors, young artists, young financial analysts. Angst and ambition. Raymond wondered whether he had a "thing" for twenty-nine-year-old women the way some men have a "thing" about blondes or legs or whatever.

Raymond looked at how the contrasting colors of her unitard accentuated her lovely butt. He imagined walking up behind her and pulling her hands down from her hair, pushing his fingers through the braid and loosening it, resting the palms of his warm hands on her shoulders, *then her eyes would tell him to pull the unitard off her shoulders and down, freeing her sumptuous breasts.* Sumptuous and Italian. *Elegante.* He didn't even know if that was an Italian word, but it sounded good. *She cups her breasts in her hands as if she is shy. He moves her hands from her breasts and places them on the mantel of the fireplace below the mirror, kisses her neck, and pulls the unitard and leggings down to her ankles.*

Brenda snapped her hair clip in place and caught Raymond's eyes in the mirror. Pig.

She had caught him.

"You look marvelous, Brenda." A strategy to recover. He was careful to keep his tone on the appreciative side of lecherous.

"Thanks to Lycra."

"Yes."

"For someone who knows a lot about racial and sexual harassment, you're treading in politically incorrect waters."

"We don't work together, Brenda. I was just complimenting you."

"*Hom sup low.*"

"I didn't know you spoke Chinese."

"A girl has to defend herself from dirty old men." Brenda turned away from the mirror and faced Raymond. "You should be ashamed of yourself. You're in Ro's apartment."

"I'm just the houseboy this week." He was still holding the watering can.

"Stay in your place, then."

"I've told you before you look great, and you really do."

"But Ro's always been present."

"What makes it different now?"

"You know what I mean."

"I do?"

"I'm not into older men, Raymond."

"I'm not hitting on you."

"You were hoping."

It was conceited, but it was true. He was silent, unable to think of anything to say that wasn't mildly flirtatious. Wasn't he creative enough to find a way to be with Brenda without thinking about sex? He realized with a start that Aurora was right. For him, the absence of a flirtatious sense of self meant the absence of a voice.

"You said you needed to use the telephone."

"What?"

"The telephone?"

"I left the phone number in the car."

"Well, I've watered the plants and read all of Aurora's mail and rummaged through her lingerie drawer and finished doing other weird perverted things here, and you don't need to use the telephone, so shall we leave?"

"Be a mensch, Raymond." She folded her arms across her chest.

"What?"

"Just because your MO doesn't work with me doesn't mean you have to retreat into that middle-aged self-deprecating wimpy male humor."

"Fuck you, Brenda."

"Oh, nice comeback, Ding—from flirting to 'fuck you.' Did you learn that strategy in public administration grad school?"

"Let's skip it."

"No, let's not skip it. Don't patronize me."

"I thought I was flirting with you."

"You old guys think you know it all and don't have to explain anything. Where have I seen this before? Middle-aged man divorces wife, gets young girlfriend, buys sports car. Have I left anything out? Oh, wait a minute. How about the part where you go back to your wife and beg forgiveness because it's too rough out there in the real world? You go out with younger women so you can wow them with your tales of having been there at the birth of the counterculture. If I hear another line like 'I saw them live at Winterland,'

I'll scream. Or 'Have you ever seen *La Strada?*' Or how about when you start digging up your old college books to give to us. 'Here, read *The Immense Journey.*'" Brenda walked past Raymond to the bookcase. "If I see Aurora reading another book entitled"—she pulled the books out one by one and let them fall to the floor— "*Immigrants to Gold Mountain, Prisoner of Exile: The Complete History of America's Concentration Camps,* and *The Wretched of the Earth,* I think I'll puke."

"You're threatened by them, aren't you?" Raymond pointed at the books with the watering can.

"Threatened? By what?"

"These books and by what Aurora says about Asian American identity."

"I *know* who I am."

"I know who you are too. You cling to the idea that Asian American women are different and more desirable. You wanted to be one of those beautiful Asian television news anchors, but you ended up in advertising. The guys you go out with are virtually all third-generation Ivy League WASPs who give you access to the world. Doors are opened for you. There's no such thing as a 'glass ceiling' for Brenda Nishitani."

"Let's skip it; you just don't get it."

"Oh, now you want to skip it. How convenient."

"Put that damn watering can down; you might hurt somebody. You really do look like the houseboy."

Raymond put the watering can down, picked up the books, and put them back on the shelf.

Brenda took a deep breath. "All I know is that Ro and I used to have a lot more fun before you put all those ideas in her head about identity. Ro is Ro. You made her start talking all that nonsense about being an Asian American woman."

"She *is* an Asian American woman."

"You were trying to make her into a politically correct Asian American robot."

"I wasn't making her into a robot. It's a racist world; she needs to know how to defend herself."

"Defend herself!" Brenda turned to face him. "I suppose she's defending herself when she calls my boyfriend a racist."

"What?"

"She knew Paul before you came along, and she never called him anything like that before."

Raymond laughed. "So this is what it's all about. If she called him one, then he must be one."

"Don't try to brush me off. Paul was very hurt, and you're responsible."

Actually, it occurred to Raymond, he might be to blame. Aurora had told him about several faux pas Paul had made on his first visit to Brenda's parents' home. He had taken off his shoes upon entering the house, only to notice that everyone else had kept theirs on. He had been too large, too intrusive, impolite. He hadn't brought a gift, he had eaten the last piece of chicken, and he had poured soy sauce on everything. Raymond had joked that the only excuse for his racism was poor manners.

"I thought we were talking about Aurora, not you."

"You don't want to accept responsibility, do you?"

"I didn't call your boyfriend a racist. Aurora must have called it like she saw it. Maybe she was trying to help you."

"Fuck you."

"Now we're back where we started."

Neither could look at the other.

"Why did Aurora call Paul a racist?"

"I don't want to talk about it."

"Brenda, this is getting us nowhere." Raymond watched Brenda as she sat at one end of the couch, crossed her legs, and stared out the window. It seemed ridiculous to him that he was talking about racism with a woman dressed in pink Lycra.

"Paul said something about how America's shores are open to every kind of refugee, boat person, and political-asylum seeker in the world."

"That's not a racist statement." Raymond tried to sound sympathetic.

"Paul said a line had to be drawn somewhere."

"Ah, I see." Raymond sat at the opposite end of the couch. "What did Aurora say?"

Brenda gave him a look of disgust. "She asked Paul if he was in favor of English-only laws as well as immigration restrictions. When he paused to think about his answer, Ro jumped all over him and called him a racist."

"She probably wanted you to back her up."

"Don't try to push your way in between our friendship."

"It sounds like you think I already have."

"That's exactly right." Brenda pointed at him. "Where's my raincoat?"

Raymond didn't move to get it. "I didn't put any words in her mouth, nor did I brainwash her. Are you going to tell me she wasn't right?"

"It was rude! You've made her suspicious of all white people!"

"Is that a bad thing?"

"You've brainwashed her into having a kind of racial paranoia."

"That's not it at all! You didn't like it because it put you in a bad position—you knew Aurora was right, and she was forcing you to take a stand on the issue."

"You're right, Raymond, this is getting us nowhere. It's too late anyway; the damage is done." Brenda stood and retrieved her raincoat. "There's no gray area with you. You are right and we young girls who don't know anything are wrong, but we're grateful to you for teaching us. Everything has to be black or white, or should I say yellow and white? People have to express their identity all the time. It wasn't enough that Ro was half Japanese. She had to be one hundred percent Asian. You should have let up now and then and let her decide what her identity was for herself. But no, you couldn't do that, so now you and Ro are *finis*."

Raymond wanted to compliment her on her French. "You don't get it, Brenda. I didn't ask her to choose one or the other identity. That's like asking her to choose between her mother and her father. The way she grew up, she didn't think much about what it means to be Asian American. With me she thought about it more. Is that so bad?"

"With you she practically had a pop quiz every day. Maybe it's that job of yours. You talk about minority this and that all day, and then you bring it home. Shit, Ro says you talk about it in bed. Maybe you can't help it. You remind me of all those Asian American students I met in college who were always trying to guilt me into taking Asian American studies and ethnic studies classes. You're just like them except now you're getting paid for it. Don't you know you were just in the right place at the right time? You were a *person of color* with a public administration degree when there were none. Well, congratulations—your job's secure; you don't have to keep justifying your luck."

"I think it's a little more complicated than luck, Brenda."

"I don't get any breaks because I'm Japanese American."

"You don't think so? Then you have no idea." Raymond took a step toward her. "You better believe that someone is keeping score and in the affirmative action world you count as two in the quota column." Raymond thought, *Not to mention the breaks you get for being gorgeous.*

"Ray, Ray, Ray, the difference between you and me is that I'm willing to admit that I harbor some contradictions and even some double standards. What do you want—to be politically correct or to get Aurora back?" Brenda waited for an answer, but it was obvious what the answer was. She took a step closer to him. "Yeah, I thought so. You're not stupid, but it might be too late."

"OK, truce, Brenda. I'm the ex-boyfriend, and you're her friend. I know whose side you're on, and loyalty means a lot to both of us. I love Aurora. I made mistakes. She's sorry. I'm sorry. I'm here watering her plants not because she needs someone to water her plants but because we're having a hard time letting go. I give her my keys, she gives them back to me. I want her to give them back to me. I'm forty and I'm playing games. It all hurts." Raymond looked around the room for his coat. "I'm off to work. Here's the key; lock the door when you leave. Aurora will be back the day after tomorrow."

Just before the door slammed, he heard Brenda yell, "You're forty-one, not forty!"

IT WAS COLD AND FOGGY when Raymond crossed the Bay Bridge into Oakland. Brenda would assume he had left so abruptly because he couldn't face the truth. The fact was, he muttered to himself, his age was the only thing Brenda had gotten right. But who the fuck cared? He certainly didn't. After work he was going to buy an Italian black leather jacket, an Italian silk shirt, an Italian silk tie, an Armani suit, an espresso maker, and a red Alfa Romeo. Fuck it. Prove everyone right.

By the time he got to work, he had calmed down. The leather jacket was all that remained on the shopping list. His good humor persisted until a little after eleven, when Jennifer, the student receptionist, buzzed him.

"A woman named Brenda who said she was your sister was just here. She dropped off your keys and a bakery box," she said loudly.

"She said you forgot it. Should I put it in the refrigerator? If you want to call her, she left her phone number." Long pause. "You don't know your sister's phone number?" Laughter.

How much was an Armani suit?

◆ ◆ ◆

RAYMOND DECLINED TO LOOK IN THE BOX. He couldn't bear to give the receptionist the satisfaction. Besides, he was running late for his weekly midmorning coffee break with Jimmy Chan, at an Italian pastry shop halfway between the campus and the newspaper.

Raymond was reading a book Jimmy Chan had bought in a used-book store for twenty-five cents. It was entitled *Chinese Girls in Bondage*, and it had been published in the 1930s.

Somewhere in the depths of Chinatown, in rat-infested secret tunnels, Chinamen sold their women into slavery and prostitution, bound their feet, laughed in their faces with yellow, opium-stained teeth, probed their bodies with long, dirty fingernails. The Chinamen never bathed and had big liquid yellow eyes bulging out of pockmarked greasy faces. Up on the streets of Chinatown, missionaries worked around the clock, rescuing the Chinese women from bondage. The oily Chinks ate rats and cats.

In spite of this, white women ventured into Chinatown for fun and games—white women in virginal white lace and matching parasols, lured by the thrills and chills of the Orient. What did they want? A little hit off the opium pipe. The poor wayward but Christian Irish girls (they all seemed to be Irish, for some reason) came for the drugs and, it was hinted, the men. Meghan visited the 'hood for a puff of free poppy and ended up in a drugged stupor, with a leering Chink fondling her alabaster thighs and porcelain breasts.

Eventually an Irish cop named Murphy, armed with a single pathetic pistol and a nuclear arsenal of nuns, descended into the den of perversion and despair and flicked on the light of Western civilization and religion. The rat-eating yellow horde scattered like so many cockroaches and fled deeper into the tunnel of oily black smoke. Murphy carried Meghan to safety, her once-white lace dress now yellowed and ripped at the bodice. Yet still Meghan resisted. "I must have it! I must have it!" she cried out. Her last words before she fainted were "Chang! Chang!"

OVER COFFEE, Jimmy and Raymond decided the ending was a happy one, not for the religious rescue and salvation, but for Chinese manhood and a guy named Chang.

"Shit, man," Jimmy said, staring into his doppio espresso, "it wasn't the opium Meghan was after. It was the dudes."

"Uh huh, you got that right," Raymond replied, stirring his mocha. "She wasn't screaming for no weed at the end; she wanted Chang."

"Why were we selling our women?"

"They were being sold into prostitution."

"Why didn't we just be the pimps? Isn't that more profitable in the long run?"

"We were stupid and evil."

"And why would we sell Chinese girls? Wouldn't we want to keep them? There weren't any Chinese women around then."

"Ray, Ray, stop being a fucking sociologist. It's pulp fiction from the thirties. It was written by a white guy. Evil Chinamen are evil Chinamen, plain and simple. We sell women. We live in tunnels in Chinatown."

"Have you ever seen a tunnel in Chinatown?"

"Isn't it better to be evil and Chinky than sexless and obsequious?"

"Remember Fu Manchu's daughter? She was a nymphomaniac. She never made it with China boys, though. She was always reserved for some kind of revenge thing enacted upon some poor white boy. Old Fu tries to torture his captives by giving them to his daughter. I remember saying to the television, 'I'll take her.'"

"They don't make Chinese girls like that anymore."

"What was her name?"

"Fu something."

"Remember Angela Fu, from high school?" Jimmy got a gleam in his eye. "Oh, man, Ding, she was always sitting right behind you. She had it for you big time."

"She sat there because she came after me in the alphabet."

"She used to lean over and ask you questions and push those tits up against your shoulder."

"You were pretty observant."

Jimmy leaned forward and whispered, "When she'd sit back after leaning all over you, her nipples would be all erect."

"Stop it."

"She was a legend. Let's call her up."

"She's a math professor at MIT."

"Let's call her up."

"She's married and has two children."

"Let's call her up."

"Her husband is a physicist."

"Her nipples?"

"Maybe we should call her up."

"The evil Chinamen rise up from their opium dens and go to MIT."

"You're forgetting. We don't need to go to MIT; Irish women come to us."

"I like Irish women. They smell like Irish Spring."

Raymond pointed at Jimmy's espresso. "Don't let that liquid

chandu go to your head. You're a married man, Jimmy." Raymond took a sip of his mocha. "Aurora called me the other day."

"Oh, shit, man! Every time you order a mocha with whipped cream, you start talking about Aurora. Must be some kind of Pavlovian dog thing." Raymond stared at his cup. He had never told Jimmy about the whipped cream and Aurora. But reporters got paid for making connections.

"She wanted to know what was the difference between sleeping with an Asian woman and sleeping with a white woman."

"A sucker punch!" Jimmy looked concerned. "You didn't answer, did you?"

Raymond nodded, then shrugged. "I didn't want to answer, but she kept pressing me."

"Why didn't she ask some white guy, instead of yanking on your short hairs?"

Raymond shrugged again and pushed the whipped cream down into the coffee with his spoon. "She took me by surprise. I hadn't heard from her in a month or so."

"What did she want?"

"I'm not sure."

"Was it her way of asking if you were sleeping around with white women now?"

"Your mind works in strange ways, Jimmy."

"No, man, think about it. She calls you out of the blue and asks you this outrageous question."

"You could be right."

"Man, you need help. That bitch friend of hers probably put her up to it. What's her name?"

"Brenda."

"Brenda probably set up the sucker punch."

"She's not so bad."

"You talk to her!"

"I talk to her every now and then."

"Why?"

"I don't know why."

"You're hoping."

"Yeah, maybe I am."

"It'll never happen." Jimmy sighed. "Jeez, for a bureaucrat you make some lousy decisions." He looked at Raymond. "So what did you tell her?"

Raymond regretted bringing up the topic. He didn't want to talk about Aurora. He began to hurt all over again.

"I tried to dodge the question by saying that every woman is different." He waved his spoon.

"Oh, shit, man. You said 'every.' Did she ask how many?"

"No. She really wanted to know whether race had anything to do with making love."

"This is perverted. No wonder you guys broke up. You should have stuck with the whipped cream. Just give me the short version. I don't want to hear all the gruesome details."

"I told her I was always surprised at how much Asian women enjoy sex."

"Oh, shit, man!" Jimmy took a sip of his espresso. "What did she say?"

"She said I was being honest."

"That was it?"

"Yeah, that was it."

"Well, how about telling me what you didn't tell her?"

"About what?"

"You know, ol' Kemo sabe, about white women and sucking things and all."

"Shit, Jimmy. Eat your cake."

"You know Asian women and white women are different in bed. So let's talk."

"They're not different. It's the man's perspective that's different. It's the cultural baggage we bring to the bed that makes it different. Everything from thinking you're about to climb in bed with your sister if she's Asian to succumbing to media brainwashing by lusting after blondes because you believe them to be the ideal American beauty."

Jimmy pointed his fork at Raymond. "I ask for sucking and fucking stories, and you give me sociology."

"Well, you tell me what you would have said."

"About what?"

"About the difference between making love with a white woman and an Asian woman."

Jimmy laughed and took a bite of his cake, then another sip of espresso. "I wouldn't know."

"You'd play dumb?"

"No; I wouldn't know."

"What do you mean, you wouldn't know?"

"I've never done the big nasty with a white girl."

"You what!"

"Never."

"You liar."

"I guess you could say I'm a virgin, of sorts."

WHEN RAYMOND GOT BACK to the office, the receptionist was gone. He made for the kitchen and opened the refrigerator. Inside was a bakery box filled with assorted Italian pastries and a card that read: "When I get mad, I go shopping and eat desserts. Sorry for the barbs about middle-aged men. Brenda." Folded inside the card was a newspaper article from the National Asian American Weekly and Raymond's name circled in red ink, and in the margin Brenda had written, "Good work!"

Miss Chinatown USA Abdicates the Throne
Charges Sexism in Hong Kong Pageant

By James Chan

SAN FRANCISCO—Officials connected to the Miss Chinatown USA pageant announced today that Nadine Hing, 22, was stepping down as Miss Chinatown USA and turning the crown over to First Runner-up Trisha Tsang, 19, who will be competing in the worldwide Miss Chinatown pageant in Hong Kong later this month. In a separate statement, Hing cited the sexist nature of the judging in the Hong Kong pageant as the reason for her decision to abdicate the title. A graduate in sociology from Jack London College, Hing apologized to the Chinese community, but denounced the requirement that contestants jump rope and perform the talent competition in swimsuits, and the public announcement of candidates' waist, bust, and hip measurements. The Hong Kong pageant attracts contestants from all over the world, including Australia, Taiwan, Canada, the People's Republic of China, as well as the U.S. Hing noted that the Miss Chinatown pageants in American cities were all "scholarship pageants" and it was an honor to have competed and to have won the title of Miss Chinatown USA. Tsang, a student at Rice University in Houston, said from her home, "I am thrilled and honored to have the chance to represent my community at the pageant." Pageant officials would not comment on whether Hing would have to return her winnings, totaling over $25,000 in cash and other prizes. A San Francisco pageant official who spoke on condition of anonymity noted that "Miss Hing was never comfortable wearing the crown, but we have a long tradition that needs to be protected. We are not dehumanizing women, we are giving them opportunities." Raymond Ding, assistant director of the Office of Minority Affairs at Jack London College, who is himself Chinese American and who was acquainted with Hing as a student, said, "[Hing] was defining herself as a woman of the '90s and must have felt her identity and pride was worth more than cash and mink coats."

◆ ◆ ◆

"How much do you know about this car, Mr. Ding?"

"Oh, I've shopped around here and there."

"Have you owned one before?"

"No."

"What are you driving now?"

"A Toyota."

"Reliable car. Are you interested in trading it in?"

"Perhaps. Depending on the deal, you know."

"Is that the Toyota parked at the curb?"

"That's it."

"To be honest, you might be better off just keeping it and selling it on your own."

"Sure, why not."

"If you don't mind me saying, sir, that's a beautiful suit you're wearing. Is it an Armani?"

"Yes, it is."

"Well, we can complete your wardrobe with this Italian beauty. Black leather interior. The convertible top is an easy one-handed operation."

"Very nice."

"Let's pop the hood and look at the engine. There. You know what you're looking at?"

"The engine."

"I'm sure I don't have to tell you about the fuel-injected, double-overhead-cam, all-aluminum engine mated to a five-speed transmission."

"No, you don't."

"After we go for a spin, what do you think it will take for us to make a deal, sir?"

"Do you have it in red?"

9 pathology

A DREAM ABOUT MAKING LOVE DISTURBED AURORA IN her sleep. It was still dark. She knew without looking that she hadn't slept long. She rarely dreamed about having sex. Who was she with? Were they in bed or somewhere else? Was it Bill? Bill was sound asleep, his back turned to her. Aurora turned away from him and climbed out of bed. She was naked. She picked up her bathrobe from the floor and checked the clock. Ten after two. She and Bill had made love only two hours earlier. She was wet. Had she dreamed about making love with him? Was she wet from the dream? "Is it real or is it Memorex?" she asked herself, and with the sarcasm, the delicate moment and the memory were gone. She looked at Bill again and said aloud in the dark, "That was funny, William." No answer.

Bill was best friends with Brenda's boyfriend, Paul. Brenda was delighted that Aurora and Bill had gotten together, because it signaled that "things were getting back to normal." Two white guys was normal, and normality meant that Aurora was getting back to being the old Aurora, before Raymond.

Bill had been there when Aurora called Paul a racist. He didn't try to defend his friend but instead offered Aurora a ride home and in the car asked her to explain why. She waited for him to say the predictable things about her being hypersensitive or overreacting, the things she used to say to Raymond when they argued. She waited for him to defend his friend, but he didn't. Instead he listened.

With nothing to lose, Aurora launched into a lecture.

"First of all, don't use the term 'Oriental.' I'm not a rug. I'm Asian or Asian American. You wouldn't call African Americans Negroes anymore."

He agreed and thanked her for taking the time to explain. But he added, "I'd rather call you Aurora."

For a white guy, he wasn't bad. He was her age and worked selling mutual funds and other investments. Aurora told her mother about Bill, and her mother told her father, and things seemed normal again. She was relaxed around him. The word "return" occurred to Aurora. Bill was a return to the familiar. Even the way he looked was familiar to her, a return to the wholesome midwestern guys she had grown up with, even though Bill was from San Diego. His father was also a career navy man, but an officer. Bill was slightly over six feet tall and muscular, yet limber and flexible. He was worried about not working out, being thirty, buying a new car, getting a better job. There were no political challenges to surmount, concepts to be swallowed, or action to be taken. There were no issues between them except personal ones.

"Are we in love?" Aurora asked Bill.

"I'm crazy about you," Bill answered. "I've never known anyone more beautiful than you." This was the way lovers were supposed to speak.

There were a lot of things Bill said that Raymond never said, and this was a comfort to Aurora. Bill didn't talk ethnic identity, didn't ask Aurora a lot of questions of any kind. Bill talked vacations: Hawaii, New Zealand, Mexico, Paris, Rome. Paul, Brenda, Bill, and Aurora went to Paris, where they stayed at a little hotel in the

Marais. Paul thought he could speak French, but the French pretended they didn't understand him. The four of them intentionally spoke bad French after that. French people complimented Brenda on her English.

While sitting in the courtyard of the Picasso Museum, waiting for it to open, the four of them talked about marriage. Not in a specific or personal way, just the theory of it.

"This is the most romantic city I've ever been to," Brenda said.

"This is where you go on your honeymoon," Paul added.

"Are you two trying to tell us something?" Aurora asked.

Brenda laughed. "No, Ro."

"This is not a honeymoon city," Bill said. "This is where you meet the person you eventually marry."

They all hummed an out-of-harmony agreement, each of them privately reflecting on whether this moment, in the courtyard of the Picasso Museum, would turn out to be a significant moment in their personal histories or just another vacation with just another lover. Brenda looked at Paul, and Bill looked at Aurora. Maybe eye contact would tell what was possible.

"Marriage," Aurora began. "Whew."

"Yeah," Paul added.

Bill laughed. "Let's not all get nervous. I was just thinking about all those movies where people fall in love in Paris and live happily ever after."

"My buddy the film critic." Paul sounded relieved.

Brenda and Aurora sensed his relief and eyed each other. Brenda stood and pointed. "There's my husband now." A white-haired old man was walking beside his bicycle. In the basket on the front of the bike were a bouquet of flowers and a dachshund "You guys go on in; I'm spending the rest of my life with Pierre."

Paul pulled her to him. "I vill keel him eef he tooches my vooman."

It struck Aurora that this was the way people her age spoke. Had she become one of those younger women who preferred older men? Not that she knew what those women were like. Did they want to feel more secure, or were they simply less self-reliant, less willing to forge a future for themselves? What did Bill give her that Raymond did not? He asked for her advice. He asked for her help. She had even loaned him money for the vacation.

"How many more days do we have here?" Aurora asked.

AT CHRISTMAS THEY WENT TO MAUI. They rented a condo and joked about playing house. Bill and Paul did all the cooking to make it a real vacation for Brenda and Aurora. Aurora had balked at the idea of going to Hawaii because she had been there with Raymond.

They had gone to Kauai, where she was instantly and entirely comfortable. Locals thought she was one of them. In Hawaii she had learned she was *hapa*, half. Being *hapa* was desirable in Hawaii—or, to be politically correct, Hawai'i. In Kaua'i even Raymond was looked upon with some skepticism, since it was obvious he was a "mainland Asian" or *pake*, Chinese. Locals could tell Aurora didn't live there, but they assumed she was from Hawai'i and had simply gone away for a while. Aurora *belonged*. In San Francisco, being with Raymond meant belonging and not having to explain herself, but in Hawai'i Aurora could belong and not have to explain *and* be independent of Raymond's identity and of his definitions of identity. In Hawai'i Raymond was the outsider. Some Hawaiians even mistook him for a Japanese tourist. No tan. Brand-new T-shirt with printing on the front. It was probably better being mistaken for a Japanese tourist than for what he was, a middle-class mainland *pake* intellectual.

Where Kaua'i had been undeveloped parkland, Maui was an overcrowded party island dedicated to keeping tourists occupied with activities every minute of the day. Aurora had read that there were three thousand more registered rental cars for the tourists on Maui than the official resident population. Coming back to Hawai'i made her remember the things Raymond had said about interracial couples, about being "just another yellow girl in the arms of a white guy." Paul had been to Maui before with his family and knew people who gave them access to private beaches and tips on where to get away from the other tourists. But in those remote places, Aurora felt the stares of locals who thought she was playing around with a couple of frat boys in a rented Jeep on semester break and taking them to private beaches that only the local people knew about.

Maui was unsettling to Aurora. She did not know how to act. She drifted away from the group at times, without announcing where she was going. Was it about feeling out of place where she had once belonged? Was it about Bill? Was it about Raymond? She sat on the beach near their hotel and watched the waves. Brenda had remarked, "This is the way things should be." Bill and Aurora. Paul and Brenda. The symmetry made sense. Had they gone to Italy instead, as they had discussed at one point, Aurora might have agreed.

"What are you listening to?" Bill said, pointing at the Walkman in her hand. He was standing in front of Aurora, with the sunset at his back.

She raised her hand to block the sun from her eyes. If this relationship ended, who would be the victim?

Bill handed Aurora her sweatshirt. "It's getting cool. I thought you might need this."

Aurora wrapped it around her shoulders and removed her headphones.

"Miles Davis," she answered.

"Early Miles or late Miles?" Bill sat down at her feet and looked out at the ocean. He pointed at the island in the distance and said, "Molokai?"

Aurora shook her head. "Lana'i."

Bill nodded. "I get turned around here." He pushed his hand into the warm sand and held her foot buried there. "We were wondering where you went."

AURORA CARRIED HER SILENCE TO BED.

"Is it something I said, Ro?" Bill asked in the dark. The windows were open, and the trade winds cooled the room.

"It's not you."

They were both lying on top of the bed. Bill was dressed only in his boxer shorts, and Aurora was wearing a T-shirt. He turned toward her and propped himself up on his elbow. For a while they were silent, then Bill placed his hand on Aurora's stomach. She felt the heat of his palm through the fabric of her shirt.

"I don't feel like I'm on vacation, Bill," Aurora said as she moved her hand to his. "I don't know why. I love Hawai'i."

"You came here with Ray."

Bill wasn't dumb. It was his business to recognize trends and tendencies. Fluctuations of the heart.

"That doesn't have anything to do with it." The denial hung in the air. "Hawai'i means something else to me. I'm not a good tourist here. I think sometimes I could live here." Belonging, acceptance, denial, rejection. Aurora could not articulate what might connect these elements and lead her to call these islands home.

"I don't understand, Ro."

"I'm not asking you to." Aurora pushed his hand down between her legs. "It's not you."

"I love you." He pushed her T-shirt up and took a nipple in his mouth.

"I know you do."

"We're on a deserted island." Bill licked the underside of her breast, cupped his hand around her other breast and fingered the nipple. "It's night, but it's very humid. There's a full moon casting a white light on our naked bodies." Bill pulled her hand down to his hard cock. "The ocean is lapping at our feet."

"Stop it, Bill."

"The coconut trees—"

"Stop it." She let go of him and pushed her hand down between his lips and her breast.

"I thought you wanted to make love."

"Stop the story. I don't want to hear the story."

He kissed her behind her ear and whispered, "You just want to fuck?"

"Yes."

THE NEXT DAY AT LUNCHTIME, Paul and Bill put on a hula show for Brenda and Aurora, complete with grass skirts, coconut shell bras, leis, and toy ukuleles. The women were seated and served drinks in mugs the shape of Buddhas, decorated with cocktail umbrellas. Toward the end of the hula number, Brenda and Aurora realized Bill and Paul weren't wearing any underwear, and they leaped from the couch, trying to stuff dollar bills into the grass skirts and laughing so hard they were crying.

Late that afternoon, Brenda and Aurora were seated side by side in their beach chairs, watching Paul and Bill body-surf with boogie boards alongside local boys a third their age.

"We're getting back to normal, aren't we?"

"I hate it when you're right, Brenda."

"What a relief you're finally listening to me."

Aurora reached over and rested her hand on Brenda's arm. "I'm not sure where I go from here."

"That's the point, Ro—you don't *have* to go anywhere or be

anything. You just have fun. Have a drink. We're on vacation."
Brenda pointed at her mug and waited for the message to sink in.
Then she asked, "Have you heard from Raymond lately?"

Aurora shook her head. "I thought you wanted normality, Brenda." She nodded in the direction of Paul and Bill.

"I do. But you have to admit, sometimes it's fun to talk about the
old guy." Brenda paused, then said, "I heard he was seeing a
Vietnamese woman."

Aurora nodded. Why didn't it hurt to acknowledge this?

"I guess it kind of makes sense."

"How, Brenda?"

"She's his age."

But Aurora knew what Brenda was thinking: *She's one hundred
percent Asian.*

"Did I ever tell you Raymond and I had a big argument in your
apartment when you were in Minneapolis?" Brenda asked.

Aurora nodded.

"I felt bad about that."

Aurora nodded.

"In the end, he meant well. He just didn't know any better."

"The age thing." She said it for Brenda's benefit.

"Did you know Bill played water polo in college? Great body.
Chinese boys don't play water polo."

"They play chess."

"You and Raymond used to play chess?"

Aurora gave her a you're-so-gullible look.

At the ocean's edge, a grandmother was calling to her grandsons to come in. She rolled up their grass mats, packed the cooler,
then walked toward Brenda and Aurora with two paper plates in
her hands.

"My boys too busy surfing to eat." She handed Brenda and

Aurora two plates of food. "Mebbe you two eat Mama's plate lunch—*shoyu* chicken, rice balls, potato salad."

Aurora smiled and said, "Thank you, Auntie."

"Ah." The woman smiled at Aurora's use of the respectful title. "I know you a local girl."

Aurora watched the woman wrap towels around her grandsons, then assign each of them something to carry back to the car.

"Where do we go on the next vacation?" Aurora asked Brenda as she lifted the rice ball to her lips. She loved the light here. *Sweet rice.*

RAYMOND FELT RIDICULOUS, but he was trying hard to survive what Aurora called "the male meso-unoriginality period," when men tried to take potential new girlfriends to all the places they had been to with their old girlfriends and bought them gifts that had "worked" on other women.

Betty Nguyen was the new assistant registrar at Jack London College. She was Raymond's age, and they worked in the same building. Raymond's office established affirmative action admission policies, and Betty's office admitted the students to the college. They had said hello many times. Their colleagues took an obvious interest in their interaction, but so far their conversations had been restricted to admissions, percentages, and policies.

TO: *Betty Nguyen*
Assistant Registrar
FROM: *Raymond Ding*
Assistant Director
Office of Minority Affairs
RE: *Evening Seminar*

You are invited to a multicultural dinner seminar on intra-Asian dating this Friday evening followed by a presentation of African American jazz by trumpet player Wynton Marsalis. Transportation will be provided. Please call my office and speak to our staff driver if you would like to participate.

"I GOT YOUR MEMO, Mr. Ding." Betty had a slight accent, especially when she spoke longer sentences, but it was not an Asian accent. Raymond was intrigued and looked for excuses to lengthen their conversations. He prided himself on being able to distinguish accents of people from Michigan from those of people from Wisconsin. Was it a touch of the South, or of Texas, that he heard in Betty's voice?

"Does the seminar sound like something you'd like to participate in?"

"Sir, am I to understand that we are the only two participants?"

"Enrollment is off this year." Raymond had a private office, but Betty sat in an open area divided only by movable partitions.

"Have your conference organizer meet me in the mailroom with the registration forms."

In the mailroom, Betty handed him the directions to her apartment and her phone number. He started to say something, but Betty placed her hand on his arm and said, "We'll talk later."

When Raymond arrived at her apartment, Betty was in the kitchen, on the phone. "He's Chinese, Ma," she said in English, followed by six *yeses* and a *good-bye*, but the conversation continued. Raymond examined a formal family portrait on the living room wall. Betty was standing at the edge of the photo, next to her mother; her brother, he guessed, was standing on the opposite side of the picture, next to their father. Beside her brother was a woman who appeared to be his wife, and between them a boy of nine or ten. Betty, like her mother, was wearing a silk ao dai, and her long, thick black hair was draped over the shoulder closest to the camera. The Betty in the photo was the kind of Asian woman all men were attracted to. In another photo, a little girl of about two was sitting on Betty's lap, and the children from the other picture were gathered around her.

Betty said "yes" six more times, followed by "He's not a professor" and another, more forceful "Good-bye." She hung up and grabbed her coat and purse. "Now my mother has something to talk about with her friends while they're playing mahjongg. I suspect they'll be arranging our marriage next week."

"I play basketball on Tuesday nights."

"Wednesday, then?"

"Fine."

"You're not meeting my mother."

Most people described Betty as "cheerful and talkative." When she was a young girl learning to be an American, she had taken her style from Audrey Hepburn. Audrey Hepburn actually looked Asian in some of the old movies on television. Betty wore her hair up or braided it close to her face to accentuate her big, expressive darkbrown eyes. The pinnacle of her emulation of Audrey Hepburn was documented in a photo of her wearing a strapless pink prom dress with petticoats, a teenage Astaire at her side.

Tonight she was wearing a long black linen dress with square green buttons from the neckline to the hemline. Before she climbed into Raymond's car, she had to unbutton the bottom four buttons. The black linen made her smooth, pale skin look even paler. The little sports car was a bit too intimate for a first date. The silences that mingled with their talk lingered a little too long. At the door to the jazz club, Betty got carded. She remarked that she needed to wear more makeup next time and not braid her hair. Raymond tried hard later to avoid using the word "porcelain" to describe her skin. In fact, Raymond had to try hard not to bring up a lot of subjects, which created long lapses of silence with Betty.

Like Raymond, Betty was divorced. She had the same graduate degree—a master's in public administration, in her case from the

University of Texas. That explained the curious accent. But Raymond had a hard time getting beyond what they had already read about each other in college newsletters and personnel catalogs.

Vietnam or work? They talked about work. Talk about Vietnam reminded Betty of all the bad first dates she had been on with white men. She could predict the questions they would have asked by the time the salad arrived. *When did you arrive in America? It must have been tough going. Were you a refugee? Must be hard starting all over in a foreign country. Was your father in the military? I suppose America owed him something. Where did you learn English? You speak better than me. How do you pronounce your name? Nwen? It doesn't look like it should be pronounced that way. What does your brother do? Engineer? That's great. Asian families believe in a college education. I was in Vietnam. I know where Pleiku Province is. I knew a young woman in Saigon when I was in the army. Her name was Nguyen too. Do you know her? Ah, yes, silly question. I don't know why I asked it. That was a bad war. That was a bad war. You look like her. Where did you get that name, Betty?* Betty Boop. Bette Davis. Betty Grable. Betty Crocker. Betty was not always cheerful and talkative on first dates.

Betty had been to bed with some of these men. She always tuned the television to a black-and-white movie on cable before she climbed in bed. She did not allow herself to have an orgasm. She did not want to lose control. She didn't pretend to come for their sake. What she felt was similar to recognizing a friend who appeared on the television screen, but then the feeling of recognition passed. Some men were upset when she didn't come, so she masturbated for them. Sometimes they stopped her, sometimes they watched.

Betty's ex-husband was one of these men. He had known how to pronounce her last name, because he had been in Vietnam. What they were to each other didn't translate well in America, even though Betty had lived most of her life in America. Larry adored

Betty because his army experience in Vietnam had been the best years of his life. His marriage to Betty reclaimed that past. Betty had escaped Vietnam with her family, and she accepted the knowledge that they would never return. If there was no return, then all that was left was to be American. She had no responsibility to the memory of having been Vietnamese in Vietnam. Marrying Larry made her a Vietnamese woman in America instead of an *American of Vietnamese ancestry*. They lived in Texas. Larry drove a truck for a beer distributor. Betty went to college.

But the longer they were married, the more strongly the past gripped him. Remembering the availability of Vietnamese women to him when he had been in the army, he began to question Betty's loyalty. He ridiculed her college education, ripped "American" dresses from her body, threw money at her, eventually beat her. Betty began to wonder whether she was meant to live in America.

Lots of Betty's Vietnamese girlfriends were nurses, a vocation that translated as *opportunity*: the opportunity to go to America from anywhere in Asia. Others found American husbands. Antoinette was a nurse from the Philippines, whose original name was Ly Vu. She had sent a color photo of herself to an agency called Oriental Moon, along with a description of herself as "Antoinette Vu: Hard working, intelligent, 32 years old. Knows some English. Would like to come to America to learn to be a nurse." When the picture appeared in the agency's brochure, the caption read: "English speaking, 5 ft. 4 in., 105 lb., Vietnamese nursing student who enjoys cooking, gardening, and traveling. Would like to get to know you." Fifty-two men from America and Canada wrote to her, and four of them visited her in the Philippines. She married fifty-six-year-old Fred Slovansky, an engineer from Walnut Creek, California, and legally changed her name from Ly Vu to Antoinette Vu Slovansky. She liked the polysyllabic French and what she considered the American grandeur of the full name. Antoinette Vu Slovansky.

Antoinette Vu Slovansky. Antoinette Vu Slovansky. If she moved the initials around, she could almost spell "U.S.A." Her parents were able to move into a better apartment in Manila a year after Ly had left the Philippines.

Fred Slovansky had been looking for loyalty in his second marriage, and he had found it. "He treats me well," Antoinette told Betty. "He brought me to America." She was obligated to him. She wanted Betty to leave Larry. "You have rights, you were raised American. The judge—he will listen to you. Your family is already here in America. You have family born here."

After the divorce, Larry had moved to another city. Someone told Betty he had settled in Phoenix. Betty's parents wanted her to go back to school and become a nurse. Betty had explained to them that a graduate degree in public administration would allow her to get a job in a hospital hiring nurses.

"WHERE ARE YOU FROM?" was something Raymond could ask white women on a first date, or how many brothers and sisters they had, how long they had lived in the Bay Area, even "What are you?" German, Italian, Scottish, Italian, Norwegian, Irish. But Raymond assumed that Betty had been asked all the questions he wanted to ask a thousand times. Should he talk about himself, then, or should he wait through the silences for her to reveal herself? *Save me*, he thought.

What saved him was distraction. They talked about the food and listened to the music. Marsalis, in a smooth, seductive, mellow patter, thanked the audience for coming to the club. He caught sight of Betty just as he said the words "my music."

Asian men couldn't talk like Wynton, although on the way home, Raymond tried.

"You see what I'm sayin', Miss Boop, it's a spiritual reconstruction of how my mind externalizes the heart of the matter."

Betty fingered her pearl necklace and the hem of her dress. It was a relief that Raymond hadn't asked the predictable questions. The reticent Asian man was at least a culturally familiar type. But when they pulled up to her apartment building, it was she who spoke. "You know, Raymond, we're too old to date like this."

"You mean we're too old to sit and wonder when I should call you again."

"We need to be honest with each other because we work together. If you hadn't sent me that memo, I would have invited you over for dinner myself. I think we can be friends. I've been watching you; you are a good person. I know about you splitting up with your girlfriend. Office gossip and all. You don't have to explain. I don't know why you decided to invite me out. I think there might be a secret office pool as to when Ding dates Boop. We can't do this formal date thing. We can be friends if you want, or we can be something more. I can do either one. You decide."

Raymond tried to interrupt.

Betty raised a finger to silence him, then asked, "Am I way out of bounds?"

Raymond shook his head.

"I've never said this to anyone: I trust you, Raymond." Betty sighed as if this admission had caused her some pain. "You decide when we should be something more. There isn't a time when it is too soon. Two years is the time limit, though."

Who said Asian women were demure and docile? Raymond thought. "Why did you tell your mother I wasn't a professor?" he asked.

"She thinks teachers are too poor. She watches out for me."

THREE EVENINGS LATER, Raymond called Betty and suggested that he drive her to work the next morning and they have coffee together. Instead of picking her up at eight, he arrived at five a.m. She greeted him at the door in her University of Texas T-shirt. He was holding a thermos of coffee and a bag of cheap doughnuts. She led him to the bedroom, pushed the magazines and books off his half of the bed, and told him to get in and go to sleep. To Raymond's amazement, he did. He woke to the sound of the shower. A cup of his own coffee sat on the table beside the bed.

TO: *Raymond Ding*
Assistant Director
Office of Minority Affairs
FROM: *Betty Nguyen*
Assistant Registrar
RE: *The Morning ~~After~~ Yet to Come*

It was good for me, was it good for you? (You're supposed to sleep afterwards.)

◆ ◆ ◆

RAYMOND MET JIMMY CHAN for espresso after work.

"Hey, Raymond, I saw your old flame at a press conference. It looked like the white guy she was with was her boyfriend."

Raymond nodded.

"Do you ever see her friend What's-her-name?"

"Brenda."

"Yeah, that's it. I could live with some of that."

Raymond nodded.

"What is she, some kind of bitch goddess who thinks she's too good for us Chinese boys?"

"I don't think she really thinks about us as a possibility, Jimmy. She's OK."

"Yeah, she's OK, all right. *Verklempt* me, man." Jimmy fanned himself with his napkin.

Raymond nodded. "Sophia Loren diving for sponges."

"After school with Annette Funicello."

"You want another coffee?"

"*Doppio espresso, grazie.*"

"*Prego.*"

Italian coffee, Italian women, Italian sports cars.

Jimmy wasn't in the right frame of mind for Raymond to tell him he had met someone new. The news would keep until next week.

RAYMOND WANTED TO TELL HIS FATHER, but his father had news of his own. He had gotten seven "potential prospects" through the mail. A couple of the women worked in factories, one was some kind of hospital worker, two others worked in offices, plus a teacher and even a doctor.

"The trip's on, son. I think you ought to go with me."

"You really can't do this."

"We've been through this before."

"How old are these women?"

"We've been through this."

"They'll want to have children, Dad."

"They should have a family."

"Aren't you a little old, Dad? I'm forty-one."

"A family is a family. You can be a good older brother and baby-sit."

Raymond wanted to ask his father whether he wouldn't be embarrassed to have a young wife and a baby at his age, but he couldn't. Wood looked at him and knew what he was thinking. *Will I understand when I'm his age?* Raymond wondered.

"I'm not going to China, Dad."

His father held the letters and photos of the women in his hand. "I could use another pair of eyes and a second opinion."

Raymond thought that if he went to China, all the women would want to marry him instead of his aging father. Or would they?

"I don't suppose I can convince you to find a wife the old-fashioned way, right here in America?"

"How long has it been since your mother died?" It wasn't a question that needed an answer. "This is the old-fashioned way."

Raymond gave up. "I'm not going, but I'll look at the pictures and read the letters."

Wood stood at his desk, offering Raymond the seat of power. He arranged the letters and photographs on the desk.

Raymond looked them over. "Which one do you like the best, Dad?"

"You guess."

All the letters except two were written in Chinese.

"I had a friend translate the letters for me, if you want to know what they say, but the ones in English essentially say the same thing."

"Which is?"

"They would like to meet me. They say how old they are and what they like to do: go to the movies, read American magazines, walk in the park. One used to work at a McDonald's in Beijing."

Raymond looked at his father with disgust. "How old are they?"

"Nineteen to thirty-two."

Raymond flinched at "nineteen," but when he looked at the photos he couldn't tell which were older and which younger. They all looked like the foreign students at school. He picked one photo. The "prospect" was standing on a little bridge in a park, holding an umbrella over her shoulder. In the background, someone was rowing a boat. She was wearing a white skirt hemmed just below the knees, red pumps, a red sweater, probably cashmere, and a pink scarf around her neck. She looked coy and flirtatious. Raymond wondered if a boyfriend took the photo. He imagined her marrying his father, then murdering him and sending for her boyfriend. Raymond tried to imagine her naked, then tried to imagine his father naked next to her on their wedding night. His father's plaid boxer shorts clashed with the red and pink in the picture.

"I like that picture too," said Wood. "She could be a good prospect."

"I can't do this." Raymond put the photo facedown on the table. "What am I going to tell my friends?"

"Tell them the truth."

"They'll think you've lost your marbles."

"Why? Because I want to be married?" Wood reached over Raymond's shoulder and pushed all the letters and photos together in a pile.

"I'm sorry, Dad, I'm having a tough time with this. I'm sure it won't hurt to go and see what develops. Maybe you'll fall in love."

"Falling in love—that's your problem. My life is much more simple."

Later, while his father was cooking dinner, Raymond read the two letters written in English. They mentioned countries, China and America, and families, fathers and mothers. Neither of them said anything about falling in love. They didn't even have the mildly flirtatious tone of a personal ad. Raymond picked up another photo. A woman wearing a starched white cotton blouse stood on a balcony, next to some billowing white curtains. She had one hand raised to hold her hair back in the breeze. Raymond turned the picture over and read: "Grace Xiao—I am a Christian." Raymond added the narrative himself: "Petite CF, 19, seeks old CM, 60–80, with USA passport for visas and green card. Height-to-weight ratio not important. Tired of the usual Communist singles scene. Love Peking Opera, travel, revolution, cooking, children, and long marches in the countryside. Send photo and papers."

Raymond brought the photo to his father in the kitchen. "Here, Dad. This one is a babe."

"Yes, that's Grace. She's a grammar school teacher."

"Grace is a major babe."

"She is pretty."

Raymond imagined introducing her to his staff. "I'd like you meet my mother, Grace." Suddenly he felt like praying.

THERE WERE A LOT OF THINGS neither Betty nor Raymond talked about. Without formal agreement, each decided that past experience was to be left in the past. At first the lack of history made their relationship more intimate. But after a month or two he grew curious. He began to talk about his experiences growing up in a way that seemed to her classically American and utterly unfamiliar. What he got for Christmas when he was ten. His Little League baseball team, sponsored by Fred's Flying "A" gas station. The camping trips he had been on as a Boy Scout. He asked about meeting her parents.

"You don't want to meet them," Betty said.

"You talk about me with your mother; she knows I exist."

"She doesn't want to meet you."

"She's a mother; of course she wants to meet me."

"She doesn't want to meet you."

"Why? Because she knows we sleep together out of wedlock?"

"They're immigrants."

"We're all—"

"No."

"Are you ashamed of me?"

"That's not it."

Raymond knew the reason. "You're an immigrant. Why do your parents feel it makes a difference to me if I know they're immigrants?"

"Raymond, I've spent over half my life here. We're the same age. We know the words to the same songs from the seventies. We're the same."

"I accept the fact that our parents are not like us. I know that."

"You want to meet them? Let's go."

"No, I don't want to force you. I just don't understand."

"You *do* understand. You just don't want to admit it. They speak English poorly. My brother and I support them. There's a class difference. They would be embarrassed for you. I talk to my mother about you because I'm happy. She's happy that I'm happy. I tell her you make more money than me. I tell her you are handsome. She has your picture. Her mah-jongg friends approve. I know you want to pay your respects. They don't expect you to. We live in America now. I'm not ashamed of you. You have to respect their shame."

◆ ◆ ◆

RAYMOND WAS A TENDER LOVER. Betty wanted him to be rougher. "I don't want to hurt you," he said. "I want you to be rougher, not *rough*," Betty replied. *Bite my nipples. Don't shave. Go deeper. I can't. Yes you can.* Betty wanted to free herself by setting Raymond free. It was an abstract idea to Raymond, but to Betty it was something tangible and tactile.

Betty knew that men thought women needed sexual release, needed an orgasm that began from nerve endings in some remote part of the body, erasing memory and identity. To bring a woman to climax gave a man identity, ego, authority. But Betty never came while Raymond was inside her. Instead it was his orgasm that she encouraged, that she desired. She wanted to know the boundaries of his selfishness, his compassion, his control. In that way she would know quickly if he would hurt her. If she took him sexually to the point of complete freedom, would he be the same man after?

If she gave free rein to his fantasies and lies and taught him her own, could she erase his guilt, his past, his masks? Would she awake to a different man from the one she took to bed?

There were scars on Betty's body, and rough spots on the skin as if there were scars beneath the surface, bruises that never healed. Part of the little toe of her right foot was missing. Raymond tried not to look in the light of day, but at night his hands sought out those places. The only thing Betty said to Raymond about the history of the scars was, "They're part of me. I don't even know they're there until someone notices."

Before he could stop himself, Raymond asked whether she had gotten all the scars at the same time. His own scars were spread over a lifetime. *Raymond fell off his bike. Raymond cut his hand while working on his car. Raymond burned himself on a campfire in the Boy Scouts.*

In a whisper she asked, "Raymond, do you know anything about war?"

"No," he said.

One morning at four, Raymond nestled his erection between Betty's legs from behind. "Let's make love," he said, as if he were asking. Betty didn't answer. He reached down and stroked her and made her wet. She said, "I'm asleep." He pried her legs apart with his knee, then slid his cock into her. After he came, Raymond knew that he had taken her out of selfishness. When he tried to articulate his guilt, Betty put a finger to his lips and said, "You don't have to ask permission."

In the morning, though, he woke to regret. He got out of bed while Betty was still sleeping. She stirred and said, "Amy, please get me some coffee." When she woke, Raymond was standing at the bedroom window, naked. She slipped out of bed and pulled her nightgown over her head. She pressed her own naked body against his from behind. She reached down and stroked him until he was hard. Raymond tried to push her hands away.

"Make love to me," Betty said, pulling him back to bed.

Raymond tried, but after a few minutes, he stopped. There was a long pause, then he said, "Who is Amy?"

Betty pushed herself far enough away from Raymond that she could look at his face. She could feel him getting soft inside her. She pulled away and turned her back.

"How do you know about her?"

"I don't. You called me Amy in your sleep."

"She's my daughter."

"Where is she?"

"With my ex-husband."

"He has custody?"

Betty nodded.

"We don't have to talk about this, Betty." Raymond tried to hug her.

Betty turned toward him. Tears filled her eyes. "Damn you, Raymond!" She slapped at him, but he turned his face and she struck the back of his head. She ran out of the bedroom. Raymond heard a closet door slam open, then boxes hitting the floor. He found her in the walk-in closet in the second bedroom. She was sitting on the floor with a stack of photos in her hand.

"You want to see Amy?" she screamed. "Here!" Betty flung the pictures at Raymond's feet, then threw some at his face. "Do you want to know why he has custody? Do you want to know?" Betty was sobbing.

Raymond knelt down in front of Betty and pried the remaining photos out of her hands. He put them back in the box and put the box back on the shelf. "I'm sorry, Betty," he said. He pulled her to her feet. "I love you. I wanted to know. I wanted to be a part of your life."

Betty turned away. He wrapped his arms around her. The closet was cool and dark.

"My daughter thinks I'm dead." Betty held Raymond's arms against her, then moved his hands so that the palms cupped her breasts. "Make love to me, Raymond."

"Let's go back to bed."

She pushed his right hand down between her legs, pushed his finger inside her, then placed her hands against the wall of the closet, arching her back to accept him from behind. "Fuck me, Raymond."

"I'm not hard."

She turned, knelt at his feet, and took him in her mouth. He tried to pull her up, but she slapped his hands away. When he was ready, she faced the wall again and pushed herself up on the balls of her feet. When he finally entered her, Betty fingered herself until he pushed too hard and she needed to brace herself against the wall. With his hands holding her hips, he could feel her willing herself to come this time. Her body tensed in his hands, then relaxed and moved away from the edge of orgasm. Raymond watched her face as he pulled himself out to the tip of his cock, then slid all the way in. She had stopped crying.

There was no other talk, about themselves or their families. What they said to each other was familiar and reassuring in its predictability. *You're so wet. I want you to come. Fuck me. Tell me what you want. Tell me what feels good. I want you to come.* They spoke as if they had learned the phrases from erotic movies, but each line was a demand, a plea, a license, an escape.

He watched her hands, curled into fists, against the wall of the closet. Her hands would tell him when she was close. With his hands around her hips, he felt her guide the rhythm and angle of his strokes. The word *yes* was spoken. There was a sensation besides pain.

Afterward, Betty told him, "When I was a little girl in Vietnam, I once saw a white bird flying awkwardly along the tops of the trees.

It was spotted with green paint. When it rested on the branches of the trees, it couldn't tuck its green wing completely against its body."

She talked about things that flew. A bird. A helicopter. At last she answered his question. "Yes, I got all my scars at the same time."

10   betty loves raymond

THERE WAS AN OLD MEMORY IN RAYMOND'S MIND, created or caused by one of Aurora's photographs, a photograph he did not have. Was it the photo he remembered, or the memory of Aurora composing it? It was winter, just after Christmas, and Raymond had taken a week off to come east. He had accompanied her to New York City, where the *Post* had sent her to take photos, for the Sunday society pages, of a gala Republican fund-raising dinner. Raymond remembered standing in the middle of the hotel room, which looked like a designer's idea of the antihotel room—shades of navy blue, gray, and black underlit with narrow spotlights, heavy black velvet curtains. The only bright object in the room was the bed, which was all white—white sheets, massive white pillows, a white comforter. Even the flowers were blue. The furniture was beautifully designed but not very functional. The tables were too small and the chairs were uncomfortable. The bathtub was white and surrounded by white candles.

Aurora had been experimenting with some extremely fast film that could take pictures with very little available light. The white sheets of the bed intensified whatever light there was.

In one photograph Raymond was seated in a curved wooden chair. He was wearing dark-gray wool pants, a black shirt, and a gray-and-white wool cardigan. He was camouflaged against the colors of the room. His head was turned slightly and tilted down, as if he was about to read the newspaper folded in his lap. It was a color photograph, but there was no color. Aurora had told him, "This is the sexiest picture I have of you."

"You can barely see me."

"It's your presence. You're in the room to make love to me and do nothing else."

RAYMOND HAD NOT SPOKEN WITH AURORA for six months. He had wanted to call her a number of times, but he had found himself physically unable to. He would walk to the phone, stare at it, pick it up, and be suddenly stricken with paralysis. He couldn't put the phone down, he would walk across the room, holding it against his chest, and stand by the window. He tried to think of an excuse to call. He looked at his watch and thought of all the places Aurora might be if she was not at home. If her answering machine picked up, should he say something or just hang up? What if she was home and was screening her calls? He should make sure his voice sounded casual and not fearful, so that she would pick up the phone. He didn't want to be too emotional, too cheerful, too familiar, too formal, too hip, too wimpy. He was afraid phrases he had never uttered in his entire life would emerge from his mouth out of sheer nervousness. For no reason he might say, "*Wie geht's, meine Liebchen?*"

It was too much for him. He could try tomorrow. But then he wouldn't get any sleep. He needed to know. What did he need to know? He decided he needed to know if Aurora was home, and if she was home, did she (a) have a cup of sugar he could borrow? (b) know a good mechanic? (c) know a good camera store? (d) remember that cute restaurant in D.C.? (e) still love him?

What if a man answered the phone? Then he couldn't hang up, or maybe then he really should hang up. Maybe the man at the other end of the line would be a young resident dressed in surgical greens that suggested not only humanity and caring but also youth and virility. He could be the type to wear them at the gym so that women would know he was a young doctor. Perhaps he would have a stethoscope draped casually around his neck as he answered the phone. Raymond could ask for someone else and pretend he had the wrong phone number. He could ask for a name that Aurora would recognize as a code name, a name from their past, and when the guy told her it was a wrong number calling for Miss So-and-so, she would make up some excuse, dash out to the nearest pay phone, and call Raymond. "I thought you were dead," she would say. "They told me your plane was missing over Italy." Raymond would reply, "I'm in a hospital in Switzerland. The Resistance fighters in the town of Lecco in northern Italy saved my life." It was 1944, and Aurora loved him and would wait for him. The hills were alive with the sound of music.

"This is stupid," Raymond said aloud, and pressed the auto dial.

He ordered a pizza.

The phone rang immediately after he hung up. Was it Aurora? Raymond stared at it, then decided it was the pizza place. It was Betty, inviting him over for dinner. Things had been on again, off again between them lately, but they had both been busy. There were no apologies.

"I've just ordered dinner," Raymond said. "Why don't you come over here? We'll eat and go to a movie." He hung up and called another restaurant and ordered artichoke lasagna and Caesar salad to go with the pizza. He called Betty back and told her to bring her pajamas and a toothbrush.

He stared at the phone, then picked it up again and dialed Aurora's number. He listened to it ring twice, pulling the receiver away from his ear as if to hang up.

"Hello?"

"Hi?" His voice was too high; he sounded like a child.

"Hi. Raymond?"

"Yes." Too low.

"I'm just out the door."

"Oh, well, I—" Too high.

"You called at a bad time."

Raymond thought she might be lying, He searched for a way to let her off the hook in order to save face for both of them, but then he heard a car honk twice in the background.

"There's my ride. I'm taking a yoga class. I have to run."

"OK. Good-bye."

"You can call again."

"OK. Thanks. Good-bye."

"Bye-bye."

In an odd sort of way, that was enough for him. Aurora had not closed the door on him. She had even sounded casual. It was no big deal. Her exact words were: "You can call again." He could go on with his life without walking through the door of commitment. He wondered whether he should call Betty back and cancel dinner. He decided not to, and that evening, without any guilt, he doted on her. He even told her that he loved her.

Very early the next morning, Raymond was awakened by Betty's voice. She had been talking to him while he was sleeping. When he opened his eyes and turned toward her, she continued.

". . . because I didn't want you to have to bear the responsibility of knowing." Betty turned Raymond's face away from hers so that she could continue whispering in his ear.

"Knowing what?"

"My pain, my scars, my life."

"What do you mean?"

"I told you already."

"I was sleeping."

"I know."

"Tell me again."

"I was afraid that if you knew about the things that have happened to me, it might make you guarded around me."

"I wanted to understand because I love you."

"You wanted to understand because you wanted to protect me. That's what men do."

"You don't want that?"

"I didn't want you to have to wonder what's painful and what isn't. If you knew, you wouldn't take me to a movie if it was about a little girl, or a divorce, or an abusive husband, or a war in Vietnam, or any number of subjects that have touched my life. You'd pretend you weren't interested in those subjects and we would choose something else, something unrelated to our lives. It's all right. It's like a mild electric shock, static electricity, nothing more. I know you." She took a deep breath. "After we make love, you won't let me leave the bed without an orgasm, so you take me with your tongue or your finger. I respect your desire to please."

"Your daughter—"

"My daughter will know someday."

"What do you want me to do—forget it all now?"

"Your job is to be a part of our future."

"You can't ignore the past, Betty."

"Yes you can."

FOR THE NEXT TWO WEEKS, Raymond lived at Betty's apartment and they carpooled to work in full view of their coworkers. His red sports car with the top down and her bright-green scarf advertised what everyone had known was the perfect match.

He loved her. He loved her. He loved her.

"There is an amber light in our bed," he whispered in her ear one night.

"What are you doing?"

"It is reflected off the building across the courtyard." He showed her the oil cupped in the palm of his hand. "The light is this color and is as warm as my hand."

She began to turn over on her stomach to accept his offer of a massage, but he placed his free hand on her shoulder and kept her on her back. He uncupped his hand over her stomach so that the oil dripped between his fingers and rained down on her stomach, her breasts, her shoulders, as he spoke.

Some say the building was a monastery two centuries ago. There is a silence to this place that convinces us the story is true. We have been looking for some- one to confirm this, but there is no one. Every door along our hallway is closed except ours. We have left ours open to cool our room on this hot summer day. In the mornings we can smell the ocean air and in the afternoons we can smell the wildflowers. We can smell freshly cut grass, yet we never see anyone work- ing. We nap in the afternoons. I put a chair blocking the open doorway, should anyone come upon our room and want to enter while we are making love. Sometimes we hear someone's footsteps on the gravel path below our window. Other times a worker drags a shovel behind him across the cobble- stone courtyard. "Should we close the door?" you ask before falling asleep. "No, it's too hot," I say. "Should we close the shutters?" you ask. "There's a chair," I remind you . . . .

ON THE WAY TO WORK THE NEXT MORNING, Betty was silent. Raymond hummed. In the parking garage at Jack London College, he shut off the engine and kissed her. "All of this feels very right, doesn't it?" The sound of other car doors opening and closing echoed around them.

Betty untied her scarf and ran her fingers through her hair, shaking the tangles loose. "Is this the way it ends?"

Raymond smiled. "You mean happily ever after." He opened his door and climbed out of the car.

"I can't do 'happily ever after.'" Betty didn't move from the car; instead she stared through the windshield.

"OK, Betty, we'll do 'happily ever after most of the time.'"

From her seat, she looked up at Raymond. "Why did you buy this car?"

Raymond walked around to Betty's side of the car, opened her door, and waited for her to step out. He offered a hand. "Because you look so good in it and I want to draw attention to myself for having the good sense to be seen with you."

Betty didn't move. "You're supposed to say that you bought it because you liked it, that you always wanted one, that it was an impulsive moment."

"What are you talking about, Betty?"

"Why did you buy this car?"

"I bought it because I'm in my forties. For an old guy like me, it's a penis implant." Betty didn't laugh. "I bought it because I always wanted one."

"I've never seen you read a car magazine, scan the classified ads, drive by a dealer's showroom, or even look at one driving down the street."

"Maybe we should go to work."

"Why did you buy this car?" Betty repeated.

Raymond walked back around the car and sat down in the driver's seat. Someone from the office said hello and waved at the two of them, but neither responded.

"I thought you were happy. Why the interrogation?"

"You're still in love with Aurora, aren't you?"

"That's quite a leap, from buying a car to being in love with another woman. She doesn't look anything like an Alfa Romeo."

"You thought you could get over her by being as nice to me as you possibly could be. I didn't know for sure if you were still in love with her, but after these two weeks—"

"I'm not sure how you arrive at that logic from—"

"These two weeks you were trying to erase and forget, trying to love me so completely that you'd forget the names of all other women. I don't want you to do that. I want to see you live your life. I want to be a part of it. I don't want to be the object and purpose of your life."

"Miss Boop—"

"That story about the monastery is a story you used to tell her, isn't it? That's who taught you to make love that way."

Another car door slammed behind them. Raymond wanted to lie and told himself that there would be no other lie between them except this one lie, but he could not stop himself. "I have no idea if she loves me any more."

"You're still in love with the memory of having loved her."

"Yes."

Betty was late. Not late for work.

IF THIS WERE A MUSICAL about a girl named Nguyen from Saigon she would sing a song of despair, perform an interpretive dance about the impossibility of assimilating into American society, then commit suicide to free her American lover from the bonds of commitment as an ultimate act of generosity and selflessness. What would Audrey Hepburn do? Go dancing. That evening, Raymond went home to his apartment. Betty went to aerobics class.

After her workout, she stood in the shower and let the hot water cascade over her head. She wondered if she was to blame for limiting the intimacy between her and Raymond and therefore his ability to love her. A relationship was, after all, a team effort, and their professional politics required that they work in committees and make decisions by consensus. She turned off the shower. Someone in the next stall was using an herbal shampoo; its humid, floral scent triggered some familiar but elusive memory.

In the locker room, two women were sharing a mirror while they dried their hair. Betty had seen them before—a buxom Japanese American and a tall, thin blonde. They had the easy, confiding manner of college sorority sisters. They talked about work, shopping, and men. Betty liked it when they talked about men.

When they had finished drying their hair, they turned to their makeup, and Betty listened in on their conversation. The Japanese American woman was saying, "Judy, you're right. Politically correct men are such weaklings."

"Sometimes you just want to shake them."

"Of course, it's a fine line between being PC and being a mama's boy."

"Yes, of course. There's a spectrum."

"The next time a man introduces himself to me, I'd like him to have a marketable skill. Like, 'I was noticing you from across the room and I thought I'd like to meet you. My name is Fido and I'm a contractor specializing in kitchen and bathroom remodeling.'"

"No more young lawyers?"

"Ugh."

"No more young surgeons?"

"Ugh."

"A man who can fix things—"

"Not a man who thinks he can fix things."

Betty laughed. The Japanese-looking woman caught her eye in

the mirror and said, "You see, Judy, every woman recognizes the truth." All three women laughed.

"I've got something that needs fixing," Judy added.

Laughter made Betty feel stronger. She could go on.

But when she got home, Raymond's presence was still in the apartment. The bed was unmade. The breakfast and dinner dishes were in the sink. Raymond had said he would do them after work. *Don't make the bed.* He would do that too, and the laundry. He would do everything. He bought flowers and enough groceries to fill the refrigerator. He picked up her dry cleaning. He took out the garbage. He cleaned the fish tank. He would live there forever.

Betty picked up the shirt and tie Raymond had left on the chair by the bed and put them on over her dress. Did it really matter that he loved another woman? Could she accept him that way? Yes, she thought, she could do that. She wanted to fall asleep pressed against his chest, their legs intertwined, and feel his warm hand on her breast. That was all she wanted.

The phone rang.

"Are you OK?" Raymond asked.

"Yes, I'm fine."

"I was worried."

"I went to aerobics."

"Oh. I was worried."

"I'm fine, Raymond."

"We need to talk some more."

"I'd like to talk."

"Should I come over?"

"No."

"Do you want to talk on the phone?"

"Not yet."

"Do you want to come over here?"

Betty nodded. "Yes."

"Then please come over."

She hung up and picked up her purse. She couldn't find the car keys she had just set down. She gave up and turned on the television. Cable was airing *I Love Lucy* episodes all week. She had seen this one before.

Raymond called back. She told him she couldn't find her keys.

"Did you look in refrigerator?"

He waited while she looked.

"How did you know they were in refrigerator?" she said, then, without waiting for an answer, "Come over in the morning. Bring coffee and doughnuts again."

She hung up. She undressed and got into bed. Raymond would let himself in with his key. She wanted him to see her naked on the bed. She would tell him to put down the damn doughnuts and make love to her. She wanted to feel him pressed deep inside her, to feel the spasm of his orgasm. She wanted to come this time. *Let's start over. Let's learn how to avoid pain from having been in pain.*

This is what Raymond and Betty both knew: Asian families are not "dysfunctional." There are only Chinese families, Japanese families, Vietnamese families, and so on. They are ruled by tradition, custom, history, superstition. When someone dies, the family offers food and fake paper money for their journey beyond life. The living jump over a small flame to enter the home of the mourners. The living feast on a banquet. Life goes on. No therapy for the living. No *dialoguing* or other jargon to make sense of the pain, or explain it to others.

THE AIR WAS STALE in Raymond's apartment. He'd hardly been there, except to pick up the mail and grab more clothes. He sat for an hour without moving, running the facts of his situation through his head as if they were a story problem he could solve if he thought about it long enough. *I love Aurora, but Aurora doesn't love me. Betty loves me and I love Betty too, but not as much as I love Aurora.* Betty had correctly divined this simple equation. What was the solution?

The phone rang.

"Where have you been?" It was Aurora.

"I just got home an hour ago."

"Didn't you listen to your messages?" She sounded irritated.

"No. I—"

"Raymond, your father is in the hospital. They think he had a mild stroke or something. He was at the supermarket. The hospital called me because they found my phone number in his wallet. I'm at the hospital now."

AURORA MET HIM IN THE VISITORS' LOUNGE by the main entrance of the hospital.

"They've already told me it's either a mild stroke or an aneurysm. The nurse said the doctor on call just happens to be a specialist in this kind of thing. I haven't been able to find out any more, because I'm not a relative. We're supposed to wait here, and he'll come down to see us."

Aurora motioned for Raymond to sit, but he remained standing. A doctor wearing surgical greens entered, but he greeted someone else. Reluctantly, Raymond sat down next to Aurora.

"I don't know why your father had my phone number in his wallet."

"I'm glad he did. Thank you for calling me."

"I called Jimmy, but he didn't have the number of your friend." Aurora waited, but Raymond didn't answer. "I called six Nguyens whose initials start with B."

"Thank you. It's E. For Elizabeth."

"I dialed that too."

"It's unlisted." His voice sounded as if it were coming from someone else. There was so much he had been waiting to say to her and so much he was supposed to do, but his head was a jumble of images. He couldn't remember which were memories and which were scenarios he had imagined. "When did they say they would come down? Should I let someone know I'm here?"

"I told them you were on your way. They told me when you got here you were to wait right here."

"Thanks." Raymond didn't know what else to say.

"Raymond, you can stop thanking me. Your father is my family too."

Raymond relaxed. Aurora put her hand on his arm. When she did, it struck him that Aurora had been using the terms "we" and "us." He put his hand on top of hers and gave it a squeeze. He was grateful, but he resisted the impulse to thank her again.

"You don't have to stay," he said. It wasn't what he wanted to say, but he felt he should.

"It's OK. I'll stay with you."

"You know, my father is supposed to go to China in two months to meet some prospective brides."

Aurora laughed.

"No, it's true."

"I'm sure it's true."

"I don't know what to think."

"I'm surprised he doesn't make you go and find a girl from the old country for yourself." She laughed, then thought about Betty and hoped he wouldn't take it the wrong way.

Raymond was tired. He realized that it was the first time he had been in a hospital since his mother died. He wondered if his father was conscious and was thinking of her too.

"I'll get us some coffee," Aurora said. "I wonder where the cafeteria is."

"It used to be in the basement. Take the elevator at the end of the hall."

A TALL MAN IN SURGICAL SCRUBS entered the waiting room and scanned the people who were there. When he saw Raymond he made eye contact immediately. That meant the news was good. He introduced himself as Dr. Butler and told Raymond that his father had suffered an aneurysm in his brain. He took the time to explain the jargon. "A very tiny blood vessel is probably swollen with blood or may even have ruptured in his brain. He was actually conscious when the medics brought him in. He was talking. We're doing a cerebral angiogram and a CAT scan. We won't know the extent of any complications until then. He doesn't seem to have any indications of paralysis. We may have to operate to relieve pressure on the brain. There may be some temporary memory loss."

Raymond tried to think of questions to ask, but he couldn't. Dr. Butler answered them anyway. "Having a minor aneurysm doesn't automatically guarantee a more serious stroke later. For some people it's an isolated occurrence." He suggested that Raymond and Aurora get some dinner. By the time they returned, Wood might be in his room and they could see him. He shook Raymond's hand and left. The room seemed brighter and more open, as if fresh air were pushing the walls of the waiting room outward. Raymond took a deep breath.

At the restaurant, Raymond ate too quickly. Aurora was only halfway through her dinner when she saw that he was finishing. She ordered dessert and coffee for him.

"How's work?"

"Work?" Raymond reminded himself that he needed to call Betty.

"You know, that place you go to in the morning and write memos."

Raymond answered on automatic pilot. "Work is fine. The college is having financial troubles, like most colleges these days. That means deep budget cuts. There's a rumor that they're going to ax entire departments and lay off tenured professors. A budget crisis gives the college a good excuse to do things it's wanted to do for some time. One of the black professors in the department of ethnic studies was recently denied tenure. But then they hired a Pulitzer Prize–winning black woman poet in the English department. Some say it's a sign of the end of ethnic studies—hiring professors of color in other departments to make up for closing down ethnic studies. The Office of Minority Affairs might even be axed. Who knows? It's part of the backlash against all the gains minorities got in the sixties."

Raymond noticed that Aurora had a camera with her. He remembered that she always carried at least one. "How's your job?"

"Do you see my photo credit in the paper?"

Raymond nodded. "I liked the one of that little Chinese girl posing with her grandfather and the new Miss Chinatown at the Chinese New Year's parade. I think the caption read, 'Three generations celebrate the new year.'"

"I've been asked to bring my portfolio down to a local gallery. They might be interested in doing a show."

"Photojournalism?"

"No." Aurora shakes her head. "The other photos."

The waiter brought Raymond a slice of chocolate cake. He took a bite out of the cake and put his fork down.

"Is that an Armani suit you're wearing?"

Raymond laughed. "Yes, it is." He told her how Brenda had caused him to buy it, but he didn't credit her for the Alfa Romeo. "She's not so bad," he added.

"You've either mellowed or you're seeing Brenda behind my

back." It was a joke, but there was a hint of jealousy in Aurora's voice. The possessiveness was seductive.

"So." Aurora reached across the table and carved out a forkful of Raymond's cake. "Who's this Betty person?"

"I work with her."

"Is she your girlfriend?"

"Yes." How should he describe the rest? He fell silent.

"From your description, she's quite an individual."

"Sorry . . . "

"I'm joking, Raymond; nothing to be sorry about. I was just being nosy. I mean, after all, we were—" Aurora didn't complete the sentence. She took another bite of cake.

Maybe in a few days he could think more clearly. He needed to call Betty, but it was getting late. He watched Aurora eat his dessert and remembered that this was how they had often eaten dessert— her sharing what she had ordered for him from across the table.

Talking to Aurora was like having jet lag, only instead of time zones, Raymond's mind was leaping over months and years. He looked at her hand as it reached across the table for another piece of cake and remembered holding it in a restaurant or having her pull him toward her for a kiss. On the way back to the hospital, he thought how strange it was to walk beside her and not touch her. He had forgotten how tall she was, and he kept misjudging the distance between them and bumping into her.

GUARDED AS IT WAS, the doctor's good news hadn't prepared Raymond for the dismaying array of instruments, IVs, monitors, and other tubing connected to his father's body. Raymond took his father's hand. Wood opened his eyes for a moment, then closed them. Aurora pushed a chair up to the bed for Raymond. A nurse dragged in another chair, a recliner, for Aurora.

During the evening, nurses came and went, checking the equipment, taking blood pressure and temperature. Raymond watched his father's face to see if he stirred. He squeezed Wood's hand, hoping to feel him squeeze back. Sometime during the night, his father moved his leg. Raymond wanted to tell Aurora, but she was asleep. Slouched in the chair, she looked much younger than she was. He stood and stretched, then knelt at Aurora's feet.

"Aurora?" She didn't answer. Raymond bent down and kissed her on the cheek. She opened her eyes and saw Raymond, then was instantly awake.

"What? Is everything OK? Is everything OK?"

"Yes, everything is fine. I saw him move his leg."

"Do you need anything? Do you want me to sit with him for a while?"

Raymond shook his head. "I thought you should go home. It's real late. Don't you have to work in the morning?"

"What day is it?"

"It's three a.m., Friday."

"I have the day off. I'm working this weekend. That's why I was home yesterday when the hospital called. I'll stay with you. Do you want to sleep awhile? You can have this chair."

"I'm OK. I dozed off."

"Did you kiss me?"

Raymond nodded.

"Sometimes I dream it."

"That I kiss you?"

Aurora nodded. "Brenda says—"

"Never mind what Brenda says. Go to sleep." He wanted to kiss her on the lips, but this wasn't the time. He tucked her coat up under her chin as if she were a little girl.

Raymond woke at sunrise, thinking he had heard his father ask the time. Had he dreamed it?

"The time, son?"

"You know who I am?"

"Of course. I'm sick, not feeble."

"Move your feet."

Wood moved his feet.

Aurora threw off her coat. "It's five-thirty."

Wood coughed. "At least Aurora can tell time."

"I'll get the nurse," Aurora said. "And some coffee."

Raymond looked at his father without speaking. He wasn't sure what to tell him and what not to tell him. That his head had been shaved in preparation for surgery? Not that he'd had much hair left anyway. About the aneurysm? Possible paralysis? Memory loss? He would leave that for the doctor.

Wood tried to sit up in the bed, but the blankets were tucked in too tightly. Raymond pushed the button and propped his father's head up with an additional pillow.

"You been here all night?"

"Yeah. You really had us worried."

"How did I get here?"

"You were at the supermarket, and you fainted."

"It was probably the prices that did it."

Raymond laughed. "Someone at the market called an ambulance. The hospital called Aurora and she called me. It's a good thing you still had her number in your wallet."

"Why wouldn't I? It's your phone number. Where is my wallet?"

"My phone number?"

"Where you and Aurora live. You two better go home and get some sleep."

Raymond met Aurora in the hall on her way back with the coffee.

"What's wrong?"

"I think he's lost part of his memory."

"The doctor said that might happen."

"He thinks we still live together."

"It's understandable, Raymond. He woke up and saw the two of us there. His memory will probably clear up in a few days."

DR. BUTLER TOLD RAYMOND that his father was doing very well but reminded him that it would take a few days to know the extent of the damage. Even if there had been some loss, memory could often be restored. He asked how long Aurora and Raymond had lived together and when they had separated.

"So we know at the worst he's lost three years and at the least a year or less. And he might remember everything else except the fact that you two broke up. Give it some time."

"Should we tell him?"

"Let's wait until we get the test results. I don't want him to worry about it. You two look like you can keep a secret for a few days."

Over a cafeteria breakfast of dry scrambled eggs and cold toast, Aurora and Raymond tried to remember events and details of a year ago, two years ago, and three years ago.

"When did we take your father to Lake Tahoe?" Aurora asked.

"Two summers ago."

"No. Late spring. It wasn't that hot yet."

"You're right. We stayed at that condo on the lake with the hot tub outside."

"That wasn't me. There wasn't an outdoor hot tub."

"You're right."

"We could show him my photos if he doesn't remember."

"Yosemite in the winter."

"How could he forget that?"

"He wanted us to get married at that chapel. He even went to the park ranger and asked if he had the authority to marry people."

Aurora laughed, then fell silent.

Raymond stirred his coffee, even though he drank it black.

"Three years ago?" Aurora asked.

"I helped you drive that rented van out from D.C."

That memory was more immediate than the others, yet neither of them would break the awkward silence between them with the recollections—driving hundreds of miles one day, then spending an entire day or two in a hotel room ordering room service, driving a zigzag route to San Francisco to visit Montana, then New Mexico, then up the Pacific Coast Highway.

"We were supposed to go back to Big Sur," Aurora said, breaking the silence.

"The Fireplace Inn at Carmel."

"It's a bad movie."

"What is?"

"This conversation."

After breakfast, Raymond walked Aurora to her car. This time he held her arm. The way they walked together was very familiar. Perhaps the things Raymond remembered would be the things his father remembered. When they got to Aurora's car, she said, "You better tell me about Betty soon, or I'll get ideas of my own with all this remembering the way it was."

"Oh, shit!"

"What?"

"What time is it?"

"A quarter to nine."

"Oh, shit! I forgot to call her."

"You want to use my phone?"

"No. It's too late now."

"I'll call you later. You go home and get some sleep."

He had planned to kiss Aurora good-bye, but now it was too late.

Raymond walked back to the hospital and called his office. He told the secretary that his father was in the hospital and he was taking the day off. Quickly he ran through the day's agenda, answering questions and delegating tasks. But by the time he was transferred to Betty's office, she was in her Friday morning meeting. Would he like to leave a message? Raymond wondered what to say. Staff gossip was a problem he didn't need just now. "Just tell her my father has been hospitalized and that I've been at Oakland Memorial all night. I'm sorry I missed our appointment. I'll call her later." It sounded cold, but he knew Betty would understand.

At his father's house, Raymond gathered up the things Wood might need—toiletries, pajamas, bathrobe, slippers, magazines, and a radio. He called Betty again, but was told she had taken the rest of the day off. He wondered if she had gotten his message. He tried her at home, but hung up after several rings. She didn't have an answering machine—she said she screened her calls by not answering the phone if she didn't feel like it. He knew he should go by her house, but he was too tired. He took a shower at his father's house and fell asleep on the single bed in his old room.

He woke much later than he had intended. Though he remembered dreaming, he couldn't remember the dreams. He called Aurora, but she wasn't home. He tried Betty again. No answer. He called his father's room and Wood answered. Aurora wasn't there. Raymond told his father he would be back shortly.

When he got there, Betty was waiting at the end of the hall outside his father's room. Raymond rushed up to her.

"I've been calling you. Did you get my message at work?"

Betty nodded. Her eyes were filled with tears.

"My father will be fine."

"I know."

"I'm sorry about this morning. I was here all night."

"I know."

"Don't cry. It's going to be all right."

"I met Aurora. She's with your father now." Betty laughed and tried to blink her tears away. "You should have warned me about her being so pretty."

"My father still had her number in his wallet."

"I know. She told me."

"You never cry."

"Stop saying that."

"Do you want to meet my father?"

Betty shook her head. "I just met him."

"Let me drop off his things, then we'll go downstairs and have coffee."

"He needs you to visit with him. I'm going home." She waited. Raymond waited. "I wanted you to come over this morning, because I love you." She knew what she said didn't make any sense.

Betty had never told him she loved him. It sounded like the only time she would say it.

"If it's Aurora that's upsetting you, she has a boyfriend. She's here because she's concerned."

"You should talk to her more."

"Why?"

"There is no more boyfriend."

It was infidelity and yet it wasn't infidelity. It was certainly betrayal. There was no blame. There was self-pity even though Betty was normally devoid of self-pity, which was why she never cried.

Betty looked at Raymond. The tears were gone. Aurora walked out of the room, but froze when she saw the two of them. Raymond and Betty looked at her. No one spoke until Betty said, "Just keeping Raymond apprised of the workings of the college bureaucracy. Take care of him; we'll need him back to write memos and conduct meetings. Buy doughnuts for the office staff." Betty turned to leave, but Raymond grabbed her arm. She pulled free. "Good-bye, Raymond."

RAYMOND STAYED AT HIS FATHER'S HOUSE while he was in the hospital, as if his presence would guarantee Wood's return. Raymond assumed his proper place at home by sleeping in his old room. He found some pleasure in breaking the house rules: putting his feet up on the coffee table, leaving his shoes and socks in the living room, eating in front of the television, drinking alcohol, leaving his bed unmade, leaving dirty dishes in the sink.

Leaving home without saying good-bye.

11   medical history

BETTY SPOTTED RAYMOND'S CAR COMING UP THE LONG
street toward her building. She could not think of what she wanted
to say to him. She imagined, instead, what he would say to her.
That he loved Aurora. That he wasn't sure if it was . . . reciprocal.
That he loved Betty too. That he was sure it was difficult for her to
understand. That this thing with his father was all too confusing.
That when things settled down he would be able to think more
clearly. That he needed more space. That he wanted to be straight
and honest with her. That he needed more time to work it out. That
he was really sorry.

Was there anything she could say in reply? What did she want
from him? A few days ago she had wanted him to find her naked in
bed, to feel the chill of his skin as he climbed into her warm sheets
and pressed himself against her. Her body had memorized his
weight. She would warm him. His mouth would find her nipples.
His fingers would touch her clit. Her hands would guide his cock
inside. She wanted it to be that way. But it wouldn't happen, because it had been too long now, and too much had gone unsaid.

She had a home pregnancy kit in the bathroom, but she did not
want to use it until she spoke to Raymond. It would keep her
stronger not to know. She wanted to hear his decision, his yes or

no, not the yes or no of a plastic wand in a little box on the shelf in her bathroom.

The door was unlocked. Betty made Raymond tea. She drank hot water. They talked. Raymond said much of what she had predicted, although he managed not to sound as selfish as she had imagined. He used the word "reciprocal" but not the word "space." She listened. She didn't cry.

Some of it she had heard before, from other men. "Your life is an island," they said. Yes, it was. Why did men need to *belong?* Why did they need to *know?*

Raymond did not say that he was leaving her. He said he wanted to talk some more. She knew what this meant, because this was also something other men had said to her.

"No. This is different." As if he would know. Raymond stared down at the mug cradled in his two hands.

"I hold you blameless for the end of our relationship." She had worded her statement improperly, but she let it go. Her hands were balled into two tight fists in her lap. She fought the urge to close the distance between her and Raymond.

"There's a lot I don't understand—"

"About me?"

"Yes."

"And that's a problem you can't overcome."

"Yes."

"There's my parents, their former lives, my former life, my daughter. It's all history you don't need. I'm letting you go."

"But I don't want to let go of you, Betty."

Yes you do, she thought. She looked at Raymond's face, and his expression reminded her of their lovemaking. "You're only saying you don't want to let go because you think you should." She opened her fists and reached for Raymond's hands on the table. "I'm letting you go because it's over. You need to be happy."

"But—"

"Excuse me."

It was time, she knew. In the bathroom, she read the directions once again, but they seemed to have been written by men. They were filled with disclaimers and cautions about fallibility and liability. She thought to herself that the instructions should read: "(1) Pee here. (2) Get a nonalcoholic beer or watch television or take the trash out. (3) When you return, this tester will say yes or no. It will not turn pink or blue, indicate plus or minus, or tell you to weigh your options."

As she stood in the bathroom, she wasn't sure how broad a range of feelings she should offer Raymond: pity, sympathy, despair, heartache, possessiveness, jealousy, boredom. She wanted to skip feelings altogether and go right for the answers. There was only one answer she wanted now.

When she rejoined Raymond, she said, "Maybe you can live in Aurora's world better than mine. I'm an immigrant and my parents are immigrants. She fits into your family better than I do. You belong there."

It sounded obvious, but Raymond had never thought of it that way. He had always thought it was Aurora who needed to belong to his world.

"We don't share the same history, Raymond." She was giving him up, and she couldn't stop herself. She wanted to say she was sorry, but she didn't.

"Now I know why you protect yourself," Raymond said, "from men like me."

"Self-pity doesn't fit you, Raymond."

"I guess we need time—"

"To do what? Weigh our options?"

"Is this the way you want it to end, Betty?"

"It seems that way." Betty turned on the burner under the kettle. "Raymond, you're in love with another woman."

"We have to keep talking, Betty. We work together."

"Why don't you just give me an answer, yes or no."

"I can't do that."

He moved toward her, but Betty held up her hand to stop him. "I know. 'Things are too confusing right now.'"

"I'd better leave." He took his mug to the sink. "May I use the bathroom?"

Betty knew this: when men are hurt, they start asking permission for everything. "Use someone else's bathroom."

After Raymond left, Betty poured herself another cup of hot water, walked to the bathroom, and closed the door behind her. She leaned against the door for a moment, then picked up the pregnancy tester on the counter. Plus meant yes. What other questions needed answering? Was this a gift or a tragedy? If it was a tragedy, was it also a redemption from guilt and pain? Could history and identity be re-formed, re-created, re-enacted?

Betty picked up the pregnancy tester and said aloud, "The next question is: Should I tell him or not?" She waited. "Aren't you supposed to turn blue or something?" She remembered the magic eight ball that provided answers and how children would keep turning the toy over to get the answer they desired. "Does he love me?" *Ask another question.*

She threw the tester in the wastebasket. If it didn't offer clear answers, what was the use of it? But as soon as she tossed it, she could feel her love for Raymond becoming less immediate, more abstract. By the next morning, she would define him with generosity and simplicity. *He was the father.*

WHEN RAYMOND ARRIVED back at the hospital, Aurora and his father were watching a soap opera. Aurora was filling him in on what had happened in an episode she saw when she was in college twelve years ago.

"That isn't going to trigger any memories—he's never watched daytime TV in his life." He turned to his father. "Who won the NBA championship last year, Dad?" "That's not a good question. It was the Bulls three years in a row."

"Who won the NCAA championship?"

"Duke, UCLA or Michigan?"

"A safe guess."

"Aurora brought me an almanac and the newspaper. Who's this President Clinton guy?" It was a joke. They all laughed. His father opened the newspaper and asked, "Any stories about China today?"

Actually, Wood wasn't thinking about China. He was thinking of Helen. He was worrying that he wouldn't remember every memory he had of her. The doctors had told him that it was only his recent memory he should work on, trivial things that many people who weren't sick have trouble remembering, but Wood wanted to be sure about Helen. He asked Aurora how old she was. Almost thirty. He remembered Helen at thirty. He wanted to tell Raymond a story he had told before, so that Raymond would correct him if he got it wrong.

Raymond said, "I brought your mail and your checkbook, in case you want me to pay any bills."

Wood opened a couple of bills and passed them to Raymond, who wrote out the checks, then passed them back to his father for his signature.

As he opened his mail, Wood said, "Helen was about twenty-nine when she started gardening. She liked to read books on Japanese and Italian gardens even though, for the longest time, we didn't have a garden."

"You have a beautiful garden, now," said Aurora.

"I can't keep it pruned and trimmed like she did—" Wood stopped. A photo of a young Chinese woman had fallen out of a letter. He picked it up, looked at it, then handed it to Raymond. "I can't remember who this is."

Raymond glanced at the photo, then reached for the letter and snatched it out of Wood's hands even before he finished unfolding it. In place of the letter, Raymond handed his father a pen and a check. "It's from Uncle Ted's daughter, Margaret. It's her daughter's graduation picture." Raymond glanced at the letter, then folded it and put it in his pocket with the photo. "Remember how Mom made us move that heavy Japanese stone lantern all around the garden until she found just the right place?"

"My back remembers that day." Wood gave Raymond the signed check, then asked, "What does your cousin Margaret have to say?"

"She'd probably like to come to America," Aurora said under her breath.

"YOU HAVE TO TELL HIM."

Aurora and Raymond were sitting on a terrace outside the hospital cafeteria. It was foggy and cold, and they were alone there. The fresh air added fuel to their argument.

"Why should I?"

"It's his life! You can't play God!"

"The whole idea is ridiculous and sick."

"It's what he wants. What are you going to do when he remembers?"

"Maybe he won't remember."

"Of course he will. And then you'll tell him that it was a dream?"

"It is a dream."

"That's not for you to say. You can't insist that people live their lives according to what you think is politically correct."

"You don't know what you're talking about."

"I do know what I'm talking about. You tried to do the same thing with me."

"Let's forget it. I'm not telling him."

"Then I'll tell him."

"Look who's playing God now."

"You need to let him make his own decisions. He's an adult."

"Look at what you're endorsing! An arranged marriage of convenience. He brings some young thing over here and tries to live some kind of make-believe traditional Chinese life. My father was born here; he doesn't know how to take care of a Chinese wife."

"It's still his decision to make, Raymond. Why can't you see that?"

"He's lost part of his memory. Now I'm responsible for his life, at least for the time being."

"You're applying your standards to your father. He's lonely. He wants to be married and have a life. The woman gets an opportunity for a new life too, and for that she will be grateful to your father. She'll take care of him."

"She'll bring her whole family over the first chance she gets, take him to the cleaners, and say Good-bye, sucker."

"That's a selfish attitude, and it might even be racist."

"Selfish! Racist! I'm watching out for him."

"You're watching out for yourself!"

"OK. I'll meet you halfway, Ro. Let's tell him he invited your neighbor Marion out on a date just before he got sick and maybe he should give her a call. She's a widow, they're close in age. You know she likes him. It would be perfect."

"You're sick. Get out of my face."

"No, really."

"No, really." Aurora mimicked him.

"I do have his best interests in mind."

"You're supposed to say, 'I have his best interests at heart.' Get a clue, Raymond."

"It can't work. It's the nineties."

"I'll say it again, if you care to listen. You are applying your standards to your father. And your standards for relationships aren't exactly tried and true."

"OK. Turn it against me, make it personal."

"That's exactly what I'm doing."

"You have no right."

"I have every right."

Raymond did not answer. Aurora was right. She had the right to comment, and she was right about telling his father. He relented. He promised to show Wood the pictures and the letters, but not until he came home from the hospital. "And I'm going to tell him all of my objections all over again."

"That's fair," Aurora said. She pushed the collar of her long sweater coat up around her neck. "In the meantime, how are we going to help him start remembering? Maybe we should begin with us."

"What do you want to tell him?"

"That we don't live together anymore."

"Just like that?"

"Well, what do you suggest?"

"Now you're asking for my opinion."

"I defer to you; he's your father."

"Yeah, sure you do." Raymond met her gaze, but sidestepped the issue. "Are you cold? Do you want to go in?"

Aurora shook her head. "The air feels good." She sat and waited. It dawned on Raymond. She was *deferring*.

"I hate it when you're right, Ro."

"Tell me something about Betty."

Raymond marveled at how Aurora could go from one awkward, unexplainable subject to the next awkward, unexplainable subject.

"Betty?"

"Oh, come on, Raymond! Tell me about her. What's the matter?"

Maybe the truth was the best way through this maze. He started cautiously. "She's Vietnamese—"

"Jeez, Ding. You men. I need a crowbar to get any information. Brenda tells me more about Betty than you ever will."

"Brenda? Brenda *knows* Betty?"

"They belong to the same gym. She's talked to her in the locker room. She figured out you were Betty's boyfriend. Brenda's good at these things."

"Do me a favor. If I ever lose my memory, don't remind me of Brenda."

Was the truth better? Could he have the same conversation on the same subject with two women on the same day? He looked at the ground for a sign that he was standing on some kind of harmonic-convergence fault line. If his day could get any worse, Aurora would ask now, "Are you in love with Betty?" If he were to tell her the real story, would she say, "I'm not in love with you any-more?" Perhaps he should just tell her that he and Betty broke up. What would she say in reply? Maybe only "I'm sorry." Maybe she would think he was taking advantage of the situation, of her sympathy for his father. His lips moved as if to speak, but no words came out. Aurora was waiting.

"Can we talk about Betty later?" he asked. "Things aren't going real well between us right now."

To his relief, she said, "Let's go in; it's getting cold."

WHEN WOOD CAME HOME FROM THE HOSPITAL, he took out his albums and looked at the photos and remembered where they were taken and when. He tried to visualize the details beyond camera range. He reminded himself that he was leaning against his car, a 1954 gray Ford; when he took this picture of Helen, or he was standing at the ship's railing on their cruise to Alaska, next to a Greek couple who asked him to take their picture with their camera. What had they eaten for lunch? Chef salad and cold salmon.

Wood went down into the basement and opened the boxes that contained Helen's clothes. He held up each garment and remembered how she had looked in it. He hung them on the clothesline strung across the basement or draped them across boxes or the old furniture stored down there. He remembered how elegantly she had dressed and undressed and how he had never told her. He remembered how she would stand at the bedroom window in the morning, her wet hair wrapped in a towel, looking out on what she described as her Italian-Japanese country garden and making mental notes to prune the cone-shaped formal bushes, top a stand of bamboo, weed the rockery. He always wanted to tell her that she was beautiful then, but he never did. She would ask him or Raymond to zip up her dress. Her slip and her black hair against the bare skin of her back were beautiful. Wood couldn't remember the last time he and Helen made love, but he knew he would.

He unpacked the last box. It was finally time to give the clothes away. Maybe Aurora would want some of them. He would donate the rest to the refugee center. He pulled the zipper of a dress along its track. "Zip me up, honey." The clothes needed to be worn again by beautiful women.

Wood was not a religious man, but he said to himself, "By the grace of God I've been able to keep Helen."

Then he remembered Grace, the teacher. Wood rushed upstairs to his study and opened the drawer where he had left the photos and letters from the women in China. They weren't there. He couldn't remember where he had put them. He looked in his bedroom. He looked on the kitchen bulletin board. He looked in Raymond's room and found them in the desk drawer. Wood sat at the little desk and read the letters and examined the pictures again. Grace was the one.

RAYMOND STAYED WITH WOOD during his recuperation. His father appeared to have resumed his normal life, except that he tired easily. The doctor said that he needed to recover from the stress and strain of a hospital stay. Raymond screened phone calls, developing a quick sound bite that relatives and his father's friends would understand: It wasn't as serious as it sounds. This blood vessel just happened to weaken. It's really very common. He joked that his father had forgotten how to cook, clean house, and do laundry. He was still tired. Call back in a week or so; he should be up for visitors.

Wood cooperated by turning down the volume on the television so that callers did not hear the basketball game blaring in the background. "He's resting. I'll tell him you called. Thank you for the flowers. They're very nice." Raymond wrote the thank you notes.

THE PHONE RANG. The Golden State Warriors were playing the New York Knicks in Madison Square Garden. Raymond's father turned the volume down.

"Hello." Raymond answered softly, as if he were taking care not to disturb the patient.

"Raymond?"

"Yes."

"How's your father?"

"He's doing very well." He still had no idea who he was talking to, but that was nothing unusual these days. Relatives he hadn't spoken to in years were always calling and not introducing themselves. He faked it. "He's resting right now."

Then it struck him. "Darleen?"

"Yes. Who did you think it was?"

"I'm sorry. So many people have called."

It seemed like a lifetime ago that he was married and living in Los Angeles. He wasn't sure he would recognize Darleen if he saw her on the street.

"How did you hear?"

"My father heard from some of his friends in the Bay Area."

"Well, he's bouncing back." Raymond strove to sound bland. Suddenly all the animosity of the divorce was flooding back to him. If he could think of any more clichés, he would use them.

"I heard he had a heart attack."

"He had a little blood vessel pop in his head. Minor. Like a bruise on the brain. Like a walk in the park." That didn't make sense. "Like falling off a log."

"Oh, that's good news."

"Yeah. In the nick of time." *Why do you care?*

"So what else is up?"

"Same old same old." *How's my half of the community property?* "You?"

"Me? Well, I'm thinking of going to graduate school. I'm thinking about a Ph.D. in education, specializing in multicultural curriculum development."

Was he crazy or should he ask? *Read my lips. Do I care?*

"I applied to several schools, so we'll see."

"Oh, that's nice." He was tempted to say, "That's hunkydory," but he had standards.

"I had been meaning to call you, actually, before your father got sick, to ask you something."

Was there a school or something where they taught princesses—Chinese American princesses in particular—these lines that forced you to meet them halfway, hold the door open for them, lay your raincoat down in the mud?

"What, pray tell?"

"I've applied to Jack London College and I hadn't heard from them, and I thought you could do me a favor and check on my application for me."

"What?"

"You do still work there, don't you?"

Raymond nodded.

"Raymond?"

"Yeah, I work there." He answered in a monotone so she would get the idea he was now the janitor who swept the parking garage during the graveyard shift on weekends and holidays only. Sometimes he was allowed to check the tire pressures on the cars in the motor pool, but only when the regular guy was out.

"I applied under the special minority admissions program the grad school has. Isn't that part of your office?"

If he hung up and hurried down to the office right now in his pajamas, he might be able to find the file and burn it. But he heard himself say, "Yes, it is."

"Can you check on it for me?"

"You applied to Jack London College?" he asked, as if there were another Raymond Ding working at a second, secret Jack London College, the evil twin of the Jack London College he worked at.

"Is that going to be a problem for us?"

Us?! Why, no, of course not, no problem at all. I think I can hole up in my office for four years and never venture out. People will think I'm just another hardworking, overachieving Asian. "I can check on your application." The good Chinese son rose from the dead. The stench of decayed flesh was overpowering.

"Can you call me when you find out?"

"Yeah, sure."

"Bye."

"Yeah, bye." In the movie of his life, the camera panned to the right, and Rod Serling intoned, "You have just witnessed an accident in time and manners. One man, Raymond Ding, has just been transported from watching television in his American living room to bowing at the feet of the dowager empress in the Forbidden City . . . otherwise known as the Twilight Zone."

Raymond poured himself a Scotch and returned to the living room. His father turned the volume back up.

"Who was that, son?"

"Darleen."

"Warriors lost in overtime."

More bad news.

AT WORK THE NEXT DAY, Raymond was frantic. Where were the minority graduate student files for the School of Education? Where were they? Where were they? "Where are they?"

"They've been sent back already, with our recommendations."

"Oh, shit. Aren't we—I mean, aren't Asians considered an over-represented population in the college?"

"Not in the grad school. You know that, Raymond."

Raymond rushed over to the School of Education.

"Do you have a graduate application file for a student named Darleen?"

"What's her first name?"

"That is her first name."

"Here in the School of Education we generally file them by last name."

"Oh, yes, of course. Chew, Darleen."

"Here it is. The letter was sent out today."

"Don't tell me. Don't tell me. She's been accepted." A nameless secretary for the School of Education came briefly into focus, then blurred again. "Oh, shit. Which mail?" *Excuse me, Mr. Postman, can I have that letter? I mailed it by mistake.* "You're fucked, Ding," Raymond said aloud. Wait. She said she had applied elsewhere. There was still hope. Maybe he could set up an anonymous scholarship fund for her there. He could leave town. He could join the circus. He could join the French Foreign Legion. He could escape to Switzer-

land with the help of the Resistance. He could start training for the
next Olympics in the two-man luge.

HE CALLED JIMMY CHAN. Jimmy said, "You're fucked, Ding."
Out of desperation he called Brenda and told her that he truly val-
ued her opinion. "You're fucked, Ding."

He called Aurora.

"I'm fucked."

He sat by the phone, staring at it. He didn't have to make this
call.

"Hello, Darleen?"

"Raymond!"

"You got accepted."

"Wow, that's great. Thanks."

"I had nothing to do with it."

"Well, thanks for checking."

"*Prego.*"

"What?"

"It's Italian for you're welcome." Raymond couldn't bring himself to ask if she preferred to go somewhere else. He was fucked.

The Warriors lost the next twelve games in a row.

DIVINE INTERVENTION HAS A WAY of following catastro-
phes. Madison Grant College in Seattle called and wanted to interview Raymond for the position of director of the Office of Minority
Affairs. Raymond was excited and flattered but anxious. Nothing
was resolved—his father's health, Betty, Aurora, not even Darleen. It
would be obvious to everyone that he was running away. But an interview couldn't hurt, he reasoned. If he was offered the job, it didn't
mean he couldn't turn it down. But not before he inquired whether a
student named Darleen Chew had applied and been accepted.

He told everyone he was going to a conference in Seattle. Why bring up the issue at all at this point? He was probably a long shot. He knew these hiring processes—the search committee had probably picked one African American, one Hispanic/Latino/Chicano, one Native American, and one Asian American. At least one of the four would be a woman. Before he knew anything about the other applicants, he knew the African American would be the top candidate.

The only person he told the truth to was Jimmy.

"Watch out for the chopstick test."

"The what?"

"After the formal interviews, they always take you out to lunch or dinner. Or they meet you for breakfast before the interview. That's the real interview. They want to see if you can play, if you got good manners, if you pick your nose in public. They might even insult you a little to see if you got balls. Can you wield your affirmative action power and defer to old white guys too?"

"How do you know all this stuff?"

"I've interviewed corporate executives. There ain't no time while you're there when they aren't interviewing you."

BY THE TIME RAYMOND LANDED IN SEATTLE, he had fundraising ideas, public relations strategies, and community involvement plans in hand. He spoke to his strength, which was analyzing the needs of the twenty or so Asian ethnic groups on college campuses today. He spoke about the role of the college in the twenty-first century, when America's ethnic identity was going to change drastically. Curriculum transformation was a good term and a good concept. It seemed to threaten some of those who spoke with him, but Raymond wanted to show he had some chutzpah. At the critical mealtimes, his hosts and prospective colleagues explained the mysteries of Seattle weather ("Yes, it rains, but summer in

Seattle is the best-kept secret in America") and made jokes about espresso, grunge music, and Californians. They seemed to delight in the stereotypes about their city. Actually, it was a beautiful city, and Raymond thought he could live there. No one named Darleen Chew had applied to the School of Education.

On his last day, Raymond had breakfast with the director of admissions, Dr. Lothrop "Red" Taylor, who would be his immediate boss. They called him "Red" because he wore red suspenders every day. Besides his unfortunate nickname, he was fat, white, and breathed too loudly. His suspenders, which were stretched to the limit, seemed to cut into his shoulders. He kept pulling at them like a woman adjusting a tight bra strap. He talked incessantly about his trip to China with a group of academic administrators. Lately it seemed as if every white person in America was telling Raymond about his or her trip to China. He liked to pretend that he had been there to avoid the inevitable itinerary.

"Have you read this new novel *Lucknow Nights Without Joy in Chinatown*?"

Raymond had tried but could not get past the first chapter. Red continued without waiting for an answer. "Man, what a tearjerker when Mei-mei and her mother triumph over the vicious cycle of Chinese misogyny and despair."

"Hmmmmmm." Raymond kept his attention on his hash browns. Was there something in the book about Irish girls bedding down with the Chinese misogynists? he wondered.

"Say, Ray. The committee noticed that you are a Vietnam-era veteran. Were you in Vietnam?"

"No."

"That's all right. You're still a veteran. That's real good."

"It wasn't that good, and I wasn't—"

"Of course it wasn't *good* good; I meant it makes your candidacy stronger."

"Well, my résumé indicates that I wasn't in the army that long, and I don't think Vietnam veterans would consider me a—"

"Hey, it all counts. That's good. That's real good."

THE AFRICAN AMERICAN WOMAN WHO APPLIED was a single mother with a ten-year-old boy and a master's in social work. The Chicano had a master's in public administration from Princeton and a white wife from South Dakota and three children. The Native American was director of a tribal corporation but not an academic person. They had all been to China.

A week later, Raymond was offered the job.

12 extravagance and equilibrium

THE REGISTRAR'S OFFICE AT JACK LONDON COLLEGE WAS jammed with students. Raymond gathered from comments he overheard as he pushed to the head of the line that some sort of computer error had thrown registration for new classes into turmoil. He slipped past the students and headed toward Betty's cubicle. She wasn't there. In the outer office, he pushed through the line until he found Anna, a sixteen-year veteran of registration wars, who was deep in conversation with an exasperated student.

"Where's Betty?"

"Don't you read your interoffice weekly newsletter, Raymond?"

"I've been out of town."

"Betty's gone."

"What do you mean, gone?"

"She got a new job."

"Where?"

"Some heady hospital administration spot up in Portland. We gave her a quickie going-away party. We were surprised not to see you." Her disapproving glance lingered on him for a second before it returned to the student. She didn't have time for Raymond.

"When is she leaving?"

Without looking up, she said, "She's supposed to start in two weeks."

Two weeks. He looked at his watch. He was already two minutes late for his appointment with the vice president of the college. He had his job offer in hand. Beginning salary was $62,250. Big time. He didn't know if Jack London College would work to keep him or if he even cared. Betty must have seen the handwriting on the wall as well. He wondered if he should research job openings in Portland. He was getting ahead of himself. He tried to decide whether his possibilities were narrowing or expanding. He couldn't tell.

The vice president said he would talk it over with the president. It was hard to gauge his reaction, but he seemed to want to keep Raymond. He even asked if Raymond would be interested in being director of the Office of Minority Affairs at Jack London College—hypothetically, of course. Did he really want to move to Seattle? Californians were going there in droves. The question took Raymond by surprise. He didn't know. They didn't know. Let's keep talking, they all agreed. An answer would be given soon. They set an appointment for lunch the next day in the faculty dining room.

Raymond called Betty as soon as the meeting was over. No answer. His own office was just as chaotic as the registrar's office. He told his staff that he was taking the afternoon off—another "family emergency." They had gotten used to his absence and wished him luck. He drove to Betty's apartment. When he got there, she was outside on the street, unloading empty boxes from the trunk of her car.

"I've got a lot to do, Raymond."

"Why didn't you tell me?"

What Raymond saw in Betty's face made him fall silent. She turned away from him to retrieve more boxes from inside the car.

He was reminded of newspaper photographs of foreigners in
flight in war-torn countries—piling cartons on top of rickety carts,
clogging the roads out of town, standing on top of buildings and
waiting for the last helicopter. He wanted to tell her that she didn't
have to go, but he had no right. She would tell him that he didn't
understand, and he would have to agree. He asked again, "Why
didn't you tell me?"

Betty had regained her composure. She realized it was her new
job Raymond was asking about, but she answered the other question as well. "I wasn't sure. I had to wait."

"I've been offered a job in Seattle."

Was he trying to say that Seattle was close to Portland? Should
she ask him how long it took to drive from one city to the other?
Was it a nice drive? It was very green there.

"Are you going to take it?"

"I don't know."

"You say that a lot."

"Do you want me to help?"

"If you want, but I can't talk. I need to get things ready for the
movers."

"I thought you had two weeks."

"I have to begin work in two weeks."

"When are you leaving?"

"Day after tomorrow."

"So soon?"

"Does it matter?"

"Do you know anyone there?"

"No."

"Why Portland?"

"I like hospital administration. I trained for it. They have great
health benefits. Jack London College is going down the tubes."

"Do you have an address already?"

"They're letting me use an apartment they own until I can find my own place."

Raymond helped Betty pack. He worked hard and carefully. He made six trips up and down the stairs to dump garbage. They finished late. He offered to take her to dinner, but she said she felt too dirty. She heated up leftovers, and they sat at the kitchen table, eating off paper plates with plastic spoons. They hardly spoke. Raymond's guilt hung over them, robbing them of casual conversation.

Betty watched him eat. She watched him edit and censor the things he thought of saying. She felt her resentment drain away. Whether she liked it or not, they were now connected for life. She wanted to memorize the features of his face, so that she would recognize them when she saw them in her baby. He was a handsome man, she thought. She had loved him. Would their son or daughter seek him out eventually? She hoped so. But for now, the decisions were completely her own. If he never had children of his own, someday she would want him to know that her child belonged to him. *Belonging.* She said the word to herself and took it to heart.

Betty collected the plates. When she came back to the table, she was carrying a small box. She handed it to Raymond. It was a box of stationery embossed with her initials. "With these you can't write letters to anyone else but me," she said. She sat on his lap and hugged him. She held his face against her neck. "You don't have to say anything to me now." She held his beautiful face in her two hands and kissed him on the lips. He wanted to kiss her again, but it was too late.

That was all.

RAYMOND DIDN'T KNOW WHAT TO DO. He wanted his father, Aurora, Betty, or Jimmy to tell him, and then again he didn't. He decided to start from the beginning. Since he was in his father's house, he went to his room and sat down at the desk where he used to do his homework. Since college, the room had been simply a place where everything Raymond didn't want to take with him remained behind each time he had moved.

He pulled open the desk drawer and stared at Betty's stationery, but he knew he was incapable of articulating what he felt. Even "Dear Betty" seemed too trivial a way to begin.

Would it be patronizing or condescending for him to express his gratitude? It would, but it would also be the truth. Raymond put his pen down and pushed himself away from the desk. He took Betty's stationery and his pen to the kitchen table. Friendship, power, forgiveness, and love lay before him.

He could write about the future, but that would mean making a decision about the job in Seattle. All right, he would decide: he wasn't taking the job in Seattle, and he was in love with Aurora. Would Betty think he was just afraid of being on his own? He was paralyzed. All he could think to write was: *Good luck in your new job. I hope you're happy. Things didn't turn out the way we thought. I'll always love you. I'm sorry.* He had come up with more original phrases in high school yearbooks.

Raymond remembered a piece of pottery his mother had made when he was two. She had pressed his handprint in the center of a clay dish. He carried the blank letter paper around the house until he found the dish on an upper bookshelf in his father's study. He examined the impression of his tiny hand as if he could remember making the dish, then wrapped it in newspaper and packed it in a box. Before sealing the box, Raymond enclosed a simple note:

Dear Betty,
This is my hand. We didn't get this far in telling our life stories, but keep it with you and perhaps someday we will.
Love,
Raymond

HE ADDRESSED IT TO BETTY at her Portland address and sat on the sofa in the living room with the box at his side. He felt as if the failure of desire, commitment, and strength might be with him forever.

THE MORE TIME AURORA SPENT WITH RAYMOND, the more changed he seemed to her. But she was not exactly sure what about him had changed. Was it just the effect of living at home? She visited Raymond and his father often. They reviewed events of the last few years. They watched old movies, and Wood remembered the names of the actors and sometimes when the movies were made. He seemed to have a better memory for some things than for others. He talked about Helen often, and Raymond encouraged him. Wood had not mentioned the visit to China again.

It dawned on Aurora that Raymond no longer talked about the issues he faced at work, not even to her. He *was* different, distracted and distant at times, as if some sudden pain preoccupied him. She sensed the faintest edge of insecurity around him. Perhaps thinking about his father's mortality had made him fragile and uncertain. His eyes were more open, but also less confident, less guarded. They no longer flirted in their familiar way. He looked the way people look when they grieve a lost love. Was it Betty? Aurora wanted to ask, but she didn't know if she had the right anymore.

AURORA CIRCLED RAYMOND'S BEDROOM and examined the relics of the boy's life lived there. Raymond was silent as he watched her. She picked up a baseball and put it down. She opened a high school yearbook and put it down on the desk. Her back was to him.

"Maybe the job in Seattle would be a good change for you."

"I'm staying here."

"Betty." She said the name as if Seattle and Betty were two cities, two destinations.

"Betty's leaving for a job in Portland."

She was afraid to ask Raymond what had happened with Betty. If she didn't ask now, could she resist asking about her tomorrow, next week, next year? She couldn't. "What was it?"

"The job, or Betty?" When she didn't answer, he answered both questions. "They may make me director of the Office of Minority Affairs at the college. I think my boss might be leaving." He paused. "Betty—"

"You earned it."

"Betty and I—"

Aurora turned around to face Raymond. She didn't speak. He took a step toward her, but she put up her hand as if she wanted him to stop. He waited. Her hand stayed where it was, raised at shoulder height, as if she were waiting to ask a question in class. She placed her open palm behind her ear, against her neck.

He began to say something, but her look told him not to speak. He walked across the room and stood before her with his hands at his sides. Slowly Aurora raised both arms and pulled Raymond to her, held him to her, and buried her face against his neck.

Raymond fought the urge to make admissions, explanations, excuses. He returned the pressure of Aurora's arms exactly. As if she had read his mind and wanted to silence his thoughts, Aurora kissed him softly, then even more softly, then brushed her lips against his closed eyelids, then even more softly, then touched her lips to his ears, then kissed him even more softly until her breath was all he felt.

She unbuttoned her blouse. He pulled her shirttails out, then hesitated. Was this the last time they would make love? In the future would he be consumed by this memory? He stopped, unsure of himself. Still Aurora would not let him speak. He backed away from her a little.

"Should we talk?" he asked.

"Not yet."

The bed was too small, the wool blankets too heavy, but the sheets were sumptuously smooth. Their lovemaking was all kissing and caressing. Raymond slowly remembered every sensation of their bodies together, slowly reclaimed his place in her arms. Did they feel different together because Betty had been in his arms? Did Aurora know what she had meant to him? Did they both feel safer and more secure for all that had happened? If he answered yes to all these questions, then he would feel powerless and undefined. *Yes.* This was where he began to fall in love with Aurora again.

They faced each other in the darkness, both sensing the caution in Raymond's too-grateful hands. He touched her shoulder, caressed her waist, touched her cheek, brushed her nipples with the backs of his fingers. She turned to lie on her back and pulled Raymond toward her. He clung to her side, nestled his face against hers, draped his leg over hers.

"I miss the shape of your lips," he said.

She pressed him inside and held him there without moving.

IN THE MORNING, Aurora was self-conscious about being at Raymond's father's house, so she dressed completely, as if she had just arrived for Saturday breakfast. She went out and bought some pecan rolls and fresh fruit and made a show of knocking on the front door when she returned. She hoped Raymond's father wouldn't notice that she was wearing the same clothes. If he did, he pretended not to.

About halfway through the meal, Raymond excused himself. He returned a moment later with his father's letters and photos from China. He put them down in front of Wood.

"Do you remember these, Dad?"

"What are these, friends of yours?"

"No, Dad. You were planning a trip to China."

"China?"

"Yes, Dad, to China."

"I was born here, wasn't I?"

"Yes, you were." Raymond tried not to sound patronizing. "You were planning a trip to China to find a wife and these are the ones you narrowed it down to." He looked for a flicker of recognition in his father's eyes.

Wood picked up the pictures and examined them. "Well, they are all beautiful, but it's modern times. You should pick out your own wife."

Aurora started to laugh.

"No, Dad, these are women you were thinking of marrying."

"Me?"

"Yes, you. Particularly this one—Grace." Raymond pushed the picture in front of him. He was eager to get on to his speech about the absurdity of his father's plan. "This was the one we decided on."

"Why do you want me to marry her?"

Raymond looked to Aurora for help.

Wood looked at Aurora too. "She's old enough to be my daughter." He winked. "Look, son, you go to China if you want to. I'm not going. Helen was my wife, and that's enough. Why would I want to go to China at my age?"

THEY HAD BEEN SILENT IN THE CAR. The last time Raymond had been in Aurora's apartment, he had had an argument with Brenda. And the last time he had been in the apartment with Aurora, he had had an argument with her. It would have been easier to start over in some new place. Suddenly his return felt ill-timed and ill-fated.

Raymond closed the door behind him and locked it, then remained standing there. Where should he begin, faced with so much shared history? The living room would be too formal. The bedroom might strike them mute forever. Aurora rescued him. She took him by the hand and led him to the kitchen. *Let's begin where we left off*.

Whatever Raymond decided to say about Betty and their relationship at this moment had to be the truth. "Betty knew that I was still in love with you," he said. Then he paused, hoping Aurora would rescue him again. Raymond was suddenly afraid of not belonging with either of them.

"Betty made you see the light?"

"It wasn't that simple."

"Betty," Aurora said, as if her name alone were a question and an opinion. Perhaps there was no other truth to be found. The name was a sound, like the shutter of a camera opening and closing.

"I love you, Aurora."

Why did it sound like Raymond was speaking to Betty? Aurora knew Raymond had changed, and she tried to measure how much of that change had to do with Betty. He was different, he felt different, and she wanted him to be different. She felt somewhat ashamed of her disappointment that it wasn't she who had articulated this change, but conceding the fact might count as a gesture of generosity, of extravagance.

When they stopped talking, they went to the bedroom, where they lay without speaking, then slept without dreaming.

AURORA WOKE BEFORE RAYMOND. Lying beside him, she tried to imagine bringing him back. She tried to measure the spaces he would take up. She lay on her bed and looked at her closet and tried to remember where his things used to hang. Would they fall into an old, familiar pattern, or could they make a new beginning? Aurora saw two parallel possibilities before them, one a relationship of long commitment and deep history, the other a short and erotic one. Which was the most extravagant? Which did she desire? Did they really need to make these choices?

"We need to move, Raymond."

"TELL ME YOU DIDN'T," Brenda said.

Aurora nodded and tried to look glum or at least repentant, for Brenda's sake. They were about halfway through their dim sum. Aurora pushed some of the small bamboo baskets toward Brenda, hoping to cut short the interrogation.

"Where, did you say?" Brenda asked. "In his room at his father's house! Like you're in high school?"

"It was a little better than high school, Brenda."

"Can you imagine how many times he must have dreamed about that exact scenario while he lay in that dirty little bed as a teenager? He's probably got old copies of *Playboy* hidden under the mattress." Brenda swooned. "Oh, the evil Chinaman."

"Only you and my father call him the Chinaman."

"OK." Brenda sighed. "Was it just a freak thing, or is Raymond back in the picture?" She popped a *sui mai* into her mouth.

"That's up to Raymond."

"Which translates to you're letting him back in the picture, huh?"

"He's different now."

"He's on good behavior."

"There's a corny line that keeps popping up in my head, but it seems to apply."

"What is it?"

"You'll laugh."

"Of course I will, but tell me anyway."

"He loves me."

"Yes, and?"

"I think it will be different."

"You sound like he's hypnotized you or has blown opium in your face."

"Before, he used to look at me the same way he looked at any attractive women, listen to me in the same flirtatious, attentive way—"

"He's a pig. It's a guy thing; they can't help it." There was one of each piece of dim sum left on each of the little plates. Aurora and Brenda always got to this point, then stalled politely until one of them sorted out who should eat what.

"He wasn't trying to get them to go to bed with him. I think he really appreciated being in their company."

"What are you talking about, Ro?" Brenda looked around the restaurant, as if searching for someone who would come to her aid, but all she saw were Chinese people.

"His mother, you know, was very pretty. I've seen a lot of pictures of her the last few days. When Raymond looks at those pictures, he gets the same look in his eyes."

"What are you, his mother substitute now?"

"Something hurt him, and I'm not sure what it is."

"Yeah, Betty from Vietnam dumped his ass, and now he's crawling back to you."

"He's different now."

"Listen to you. I thought I knew you."

Aurora laughed. Aurora wanted to tell Brenda that Raymond held her as he had never held her before, but she knew she couldn't describe it. When they had made love before, his hands simply seemed to be where they should be. Now they seemed to support her, to lift her, to bring her closer to him. His hands held her differently at the small of her back; he rested his hand on her stomach as if there were no other more erotic part of her body. He seemed to be deeper inside. Maybe he had learned it from Betty, but now it was theirs.

"*Fait accompli* and *nolo contendere*," Brenda said. After all, she wanted Aurora to be happy.

Aurora's fortune cookie read: "If your desires are not extravagant, they will be granted." Was that a good fortune or a bad one?

JIMMY CHAN WAS STARING into his doppio espresso. "Shit, Raymond, I don't know if you're going forward or backward. What are you going to do—just move back into your old apartment with Aurora?"

"I might try and buy something—a condo or a house." Raymond stirred whipped cream into his mocha espresso. "Now that I've got that promotion and the big raise, I think it's time to be an adult and a good American and take out a huge mortgage."

"And Aurora?"

"Aurora and I are fine. We're being a little cautious."

"I don't know, ol' compadre. I think you should blow the money on a white-boy car like a Corvette and go out with some *young* white women."

"That's your fantasy, Jimmy."

"Yeah, it is. Someone's got to *share the fantasy.*"

Raymond tried to picture Jimmy starring in a Chanel No. 5 commercial, but it was impossible. He tried to change the subject.

"Aurora tells me Brenda's got a new boyfriend."

"Going out with Brenda would be like going out with a white woman, without the parental hassles."

"He's a sociology professor at Berkeley."

"No shit. What's he studying—Japanese American princesses?"

"He's writing a book." Raymond paused. He wanted Jimmy's full attention for this one.

"A writer?"

"The title of the book is *Saving Face and Filial Duty: Success and Failure Mechanisms in Romantic Heterosexual Liaisons Between Americans of Asian Ancestry.*"

Jimmy laughed the way a Mafia don laughs in the movies, the kind of laugh that makes everyone wait a beat to make sure he's really laughing before they join in. Heads all over the tiny café swiveled in their direction. When he stopped laughing, he said, "The only thing funnier you can tell me is that he's white and he thinks he can get research information out of Brenda."

"He is."

"Can you imagine the crap about us Asian guys she's dishing out?"

It was good to hear Jimmy on a roll, but Raymond said piously, "Brenda's not so bad."

"You said that before." Jimmy shook his head. "You're always willing to forgive any beautiful woman anything. But you're right. If you and Aurora get back together, you gotta take Brenda too."

"I know. I'm preparing myself."

WOOD WANTED TO HELP RAYMOND buy a house instead of a condominium. He didn't consider a glorified apartment to be a safe investment.

"I'll give you the down payment on a house. A house will appreciate faster, and it's got room for a family. You can have a garden."

"You're rushing it a little, Dad. Aurora and I are still sorting things out."

"You've moved out of your apartment, haven't you?"

"Well, yes, until I find something to buy."

"I don't see you living here, so I'm assuming you're back living with her."

"Well, yes."

"Well? Get married, have some children. Name one of them Grace for me."

Raymond looked up to be sure his father was teasing and it wasn't really Chinese family pressure at work. "OK, Dad; we'll have five girls and name them all Grace, as long as it keeps you on this side of the globe."

Raymond reached for one of his father's engineering manuals. He had taken to reading them. He liked the vocabulary and even used some of the words on the job, adapting the jargon to his new management of minority affairs. Stress. Equilibrium. Stability. Fatigue. Tensile strength. The more he read, the more he came to understand that his father was not so much traditionally Chinese as he was a typical engineer who measured the world as a structure and applied the principles of building to families, lovers, dreams. Old buildings built of unreinforced bricks and mortar had a lot of what was defined as compression strength, but in an earthquake they couldn't withstand the shaking. They were low on tensile strength. Generations and generations of Chinese tradition must result in something Raymond decided was "redundant compression strength." He didn't know if he was using the terms correctly, but philosophically they made sense to him. Maybe the tensile strength and stability his father recognized in Raymond's relationship with Aurora allowed him to relinquish the project of building a "real" Chinese family with a "real" Chinese wife of his own.

◆ ◆ ◆

AURORA CLEANED HER APARTMENT, without knowing if she was making room for Raymond or not. She picked up magazines and stacked them on the coffee table. She emptied a dresser drawer onto the bed and began to sort her T-shirts, socks, and tights, then left them and went into the bathroom, where she began to rearrange the medicine cabinet. She consolidated a shelf of cosmetics. She inspected several tubes of lipstick, applied one to her lips and wiped it off, then drew stripes with the others on the back of her hand. She set four of them aside to give to Brenda. She examined the expiration dates on pill bottles and threw away those that had expired. She threw away sample bottles and tubes of creams, lotions, makeup. She returned to the living room and took the magazines off the coffee table and threw them away. In the bedroom, she tackled the socks and tights with new intensity, throwing away the socks with no mates and the tights with holes. She sorted through the dresser drawers and consolidated her clothes until there were two empty drawers, then folded the discards into neat piles for her sister or Goodwill.

When the apartment was clean, Aurora sat down at her desk and began to sort through photos and contact sheets. She started a folder for old news photos. Then there were her own: black-and-white vacation shots of gargoyles, architectural details from buildings in Paris, white ocean foam and black lava formations from Hawaii, Brenda's leg and foot in a tide pool. At the bottom of the pile she found photos of her life with Raymond—the unmade bed, his clothes on the chairs, the kitchen table for two, and an obscure silhouette of him behind the opaque glass of the shower. There was another photo of uncooked grains of rice scattered across the tile of the kitchen floor, and she remembered it was taken the day Raymond left. The rice bag had broken in her hand. Would a viewer see in the quality of the light the helplessness and despair of the moment? Was it apparent that the rice stayed on the floor overnight? That the woman outside the frame of the photo who spilled the rice left it on the floor and went to bed hungry?

"I THOUGHT WE WERE GOING OUT TO DINNER," said Raymond.

"We are," Aurora replied. "I like the smell of rice cooking in the apartment."

RAYMOND'S FATHER TRANSPLANTS a forty-year-old *bonsai* pine from his house to theirs. Aurora inherits a pair of goat-skin garden gloves. Perhaps they are too young to be found visiting formal gardens in Vienna, marveling at the blossoms, writing down the Latin names of the plants, and searching for the source of an isolated fragrance in a botanical garden. They are thrilled to discover the fragrance in the garden is hidden by planting an aromatic herb at the base of hedges. It is their passion. "Do we have this same light at home?" they wonder. He holds her by the elbow, urging her down a narrow pathway of stepping stones where he hears the sound of water. Crossing an arched footbridge that spans a narrow reflecting pool, she is separated from him momentarily. He looks at a map to see where they are. He thinks about the woman he loves—the one who is embedded in the heart and life lines of his palms, the one who makes love to him on a tiny bed, the one who is similar to a character on the page of a book he is reading, the one who lives in a city filled with roses, the one who sends him a picture of herself cuddling an infant she calls her niece, the one who speaks to him from the wrinkled pages of an old letter he is rereading which says how much their friendship borders her life, or, in another letter, how much she loves him and wishes things could have been different. He wishes he could mark his life at each of these points so that he could come back later with the memory and the knowledge of how to occupy the heart in order to find solutions, discover a sense of place, reach home, explain his love.

He crosses the bridge between them.

Praise for *American Knees*

"Shawn Wong adds a funny, sexy chapter to Asian-American literature. . . . A multicultural comedy that relentlessly lampoons the inci-
dents and incidentals of modern Asian-American life."
—JULIE SHIROISHI, *San Francisco Bay Guardian*

"I cracked up reading Shawn Wong's witty, tender, wise, and sexy new
novel. His lovable but ambivalent protagonist collides memorably
with a cast of female characters who are a welcome change from the
shrinking violets and silent martyrs we've come to expect from 'ethnic'
literature. *American Knees* is contemporary to the bone—a highly
entertaining, deftly written, provocative and moving work of fiction."
—JESSICA HAGEDORN, author of *Dogeaters*

"Just as knowing Woody Allen's characters have been, Shawn Wong's
protagonists, Ray and Aurora, are quick with the repartee, relentlessly
self-defining and thoroughly sexy. Wong spares no stereotypes of
Asian American identity, unraveling them mercilessly but with hilarity.
Though his writing is totally with it, Wong's sensibilities plumb deeper
lodes where his eroticism is informed with shyness, a tentativeness
of being—making a potion that is at the same time seductive and
poignant."—DIANA CHANG, author of *Frontiers of Love*

"From its resonant opening line, Shawn Wong's new novel gives us an
irreverent new take on contemporary identity politics. *American Knees*
is the very best kind of read—funny, sexy, and smart—immensely
entertaining even as it provokes thought."
—SYLVIA WANTANABE, author of *Talking to the Dead and Other Stories*